AN ISOLATED EMPIRE:
A HISTORY OF NORTHWESTERN COLORADO

By Frederic J. Athearn

Bureau of Land Management
Denver, Colorado

1982

Third Edition
Second Printing

This document is printed in conjunction with the Little Snake Resource Area Resource Management Plan/ Environmental Impact Statement and the Green River-Ham's Fork Regional Coal Leasing Project. It serves as support for both the RMP and EIS and Coal Leasing. In addition, this document is integral to the Craig District Cultural Resource Management Plan.

DESIGNED BY: Leigh Wellborn
SERIES EDITOR: Frederic J. Athearn

For

Marv Pearson

Westerner, BLMer, Friend

Chapter Frontispieces
From: *Colorado's First Portrait*
By Clifford P. Westermeier.
Courtesy University of New Mexico Press
Reproduced with permission

FOREWORD

This presents the second in a series of cultural resource reports. This study concerns historic sites and values located on and around public lands in Colorado. It was derived from a prototype study that is an integral part of the Bureau of Land Management's Cultural Resource Management Program.

A major objective and mandate of the Bureau of Land Management, U.S. Department of the Interior, is to preserve and study cultural resources, particularly historic and prehistoric properties. Evidences of our history and heritage cover large areas of public domain under BLM jurisdiction.

Compiled by F.J. Athearn, to provide a baseline narrative for the history of BLM's Craig District, this third edition represents a rewritten and newly illustrated publication in the popular Cultural Resources Series. This document is the first time a regional history of Northwestern Colorado has been written. As histories of the balance of the state are completed, they will be made available to the public.

It is my pleasure to share these efforts with you for both your professional and leisure reading.

George C. Francis
State Director
Bureau of Land Management
Colorado

TABLE OF CONTENTS

Introduction and Chronological Summary

Chapter

ACKNOWLEDGEMENTS

In the six months it took to prepare this study many kind people helped the author. Special thanks are due to Dr. Maxine Benson, Colorado Historical Society; Dr. Jack Brennan, University of Colorado, Boulder; Dr. Eleanor Gehres of the Western History Collection, Denver Public Library, Denver, Colorado; and the counties of Moffat, Rio Blanco, and Routt. All of these people or agencies provided invaluable assistance in research. For field support, Marvin Pearson, Wade Johnson, Beth Walton, Jim Keeton, Don Bruns, Ade Neisius, Glenn Wallace, Dan Martin, and Mac Berta all extended themselves to make life easier and more productive. Their help is greatly appreciated.

In the actual production of this work, many people assisted and provided advice and consultation. To Julie Stewart, Dr. Don Rickey, Jr., Gary Matlock, Fil Jiminez, Gene Miller, and last but not least Evaline Olson, I give my special thanks. Thanks also to Angie Fernandez, Louise Jahnke, and Irene Goode who typed countless drafts of this study.

Frederic J. Athearn
Denver, Colorado
June, 1981

INTRODUCTION AND

CHRONOLOGICAL SUMMARY

Man's use and occupation of the northwestern corner of Colorado dates from about 10,000 years. The first recorded men were the Ute Indians; early Europeans found these natives thriving in the area. The Spanish were the first to see this region, reaching the White River in 1776. The Dominguez-Escalante Expedition of that year provided Sparse information about the land and its people, but little else. The first true users of the land were fur trappers who came after 1800.

Before 1820 scattered trappers worked the central Rockies, but no orgainzed effort was made at wholesale trapping. In 1822 William H. Ashley organized a major expedition that went into the Green River country and opened it for trade. For the next twenty years fur trade in the northwestern section of Colorado boomed, and thousands of beaver were trapped. In 1838 a trading post named Fort Davy Crockett was built to serve this trade, but by 1843 the fort was abandoned, as the trade died. The decline of a fur trade in the region was attributed to changing fashion styles and the natural depletion of resources.

Shortly before and following the collapse of the fur trade, several explorers came into this area. The first men to write about the region were private travelers; F. A. Wislizenus came in 1839, Willard Smith and Thomas J. Farnham in 1840; all noted the area was of little consequence. The first true explorer to reach this region was John C. Fremont; in 1844 he brought an army expedition down to the Green River, into Browns Hole, and on west. He was on an official government mission designed to map the land and seek routes for new trails west. Fremont said very little about Colorado, but noted that, in his opinion, this country was nearly worthless; in 1845 his second expedition into the area concluded much the same.

The next official exploration came during 1869, when John Wesley Powell was commissioned to map the Green and Grand (Colorado) Rivers. He gathered much new data about the Great Basin, noting that Brown's Park was of little value, and the only way this part of the state would ever develop was with irrigation.

Discovery of gold, in 1859, near Denver precipitated a major rush to Colorado in that year. Despite the promise of these discoveries, the initial boom died out; but not before prospectors and miners flowed over the Continental Divide into Middle Park, the Blue River region, and even North Park. Breckenridge was founded in 1859 and became a major population center. By 1861 gold had been discovered near Hahn's Peak, but the Civil War prevented its development until 1865. By 1870 Hahn's Peak was a booming mining town, and Middle Park was being settled. Placer mines developed on Independence Mountain in North Park. However, two factors kept the region from growing on a larger scale: first, the presence of Ute Indians, and second, a lack of transportation.

The second problem was alleviated in 1869. When the Union Pacific (Transcontinental) was completed in that year, rail transport across Wyoming arrived within

3

sixty miles of the northwest corner. Soon cattlemen moved into Brown's Park, and by 1871 a major industry was established along the Little Snake, the Green, and the Yampa (Bear) Rivers. By 1876 cattle grazed by J. O. Pinkham in North Park and along the White River, near the future site of Meeker.

The first problem, Utes, was not solved until after 1879. The Ute Nation owned all of northwestern Colorado according to the terms of the Brunot Treaty of 1873. By this treaty, two reservations were established: to the south the Los Pinos Agency took care of the Southern Utes, while in the north, White River Agency was founded to care for the Northern Utes. A series of agents came and went by 1879, and the next to the last, Reverend H. A. Danforth, resigned in disgust over U.S. Indian policy and its failure to keep promises to his wards. He was replaced by Nathan C. Meeker in 1879. Meeker, a typical product of the nineteenth century, felt that American natives were not productive, and that to make the Indian a useful citizen, he had to be taught the ways of the European. This meant, in Meeker's mind, that the Indian must become a copy of all the "best" in the anglo.

The Utes were not willing to give up their traditional ways for Meeker or any other European. The conflict between the two cultures developed over agriculture and Meeker's compulsory conversion of the Ute from nomad to a sedentary citizen. Finally, in September 1879, the explosion came. Meeker was shoved by a Ute chief, Johnson, and the agent wired for help from Fort Fred Steele, Wyoming. By the end of that month, troops were sent under the command of Major Thomas T. Thornburgh. The Thornburgh detachment was ambushed along the Milk River, despite attempts by both Thornburgh and the Ute Chiefs, Douglas and Colorow, to avoid hostilities. The same time the Thornburgh Battle occurred, the White River Agency was attacked by Utes under Chief Johnson. Meeker and eleven male employees were killed; Meeker's wife, daughter Josephine, and several other women were captured. After nearly three months of negotiations, with the help of powerful Chief Ouray and his wife Chipeta, the women were released; the leaders of the rebellion gave themselves up, and a commission was established to determine guilt. In the end, the citizens of Colorado who cried, "the Utes must go" won. The Northern Utes were moved to Utah in 1881, where they still reside, and the land that was taken from them was opened to general settlement.

Once the northwest corner was cleared of native Americans, homesteaders moved in, and the open range cattle industry expanded. Between 1880 and 1895 a series of towns sprang up and became merchandising centers. Steamboat Springs was founded in 1885, Meeker in 1882, Rangely in 1882, Craig in 1889, Hayden in 1895, and numerous smaller places like Lay, Maybell, and Axial grew as a direct consequence of the Ute removal.

The introduction of cattle to the range provided a major industry in the northwest corner for nearly fifty years. However, there were conflicts over land use. Homesteaders

4

tried to settle ground that was used by cattlemen. In some cases settlers were driven off, while in others they persisted. Cattlemen also fought with sheep raisers, who by the 1890s, were beginning to bring sheep into the lush pastures in the forest lands of the Elk River and other valleys. Violent conflicts erupted between these two factions, despite the realization that most cattlemen did not own the land they used, which was nearly all public domain. Sheepmen were murdered and sheep destroyed. The climax of the sheep wars came in Rio Blanco County with the "battle" of Yellowjacket Pass. In 1920 the Colorado State Militia was called in and peace was restored.

During 1891 the first major forest reserves were created. This withdrew millions of acres of prime grazing land from the public domain and forced cattlemen to compete with others for grazing permits. The White River Timber Reserve of 1891 was followed by the creation of Routt and Roosevelt Forests in 1905, and Arapahoe Forest in 1906. These withdrawals caused considerable bitterness among cattle raisers, while sheepmen and settlers aligned with the U.S. Forest Service to stop open range grazing, and therby permit more equitable rights for all. By 1915 this goal was accomplished and smaller cattle outfits, sheepmen, and settlers were all using public lands together.

In 1934 the Taylor Grazing Service was created to control grazing (and overgrazing) on remaining public lands. This service allotted land to cattlemen, sheepmen, and others for grazing purposes. For all practical purposes, the balance of public domain land in northwestern Colorado was withdrawn from homesteading by this Act, and the era of open range ended. In 1946 the General Land Office, original dispenser of public lands, and the Grazing Service were merged and became the Bureau of Land Management. This organization has continued to issue grazing permits, and for the most part has kept the public domain from being overused.

The cattle industry was not the only factor in the development of northwestern Colorado. New transportation routes developed to serve the various communities that grew in the region as settlers came into the river valleys of the Elk, Little Snake, Yampa, Green, and the White. Mineral extraction took place in areas such as Fortification Creek and Blue Mountain, while hay and grains were grown to provide food and fodder along the valley floors. The Yampa Valley became a major hay raising area, while the far west was still cattle domain.

In Middle Park, one of the earliest areas of settlement, growth continued. Tourism, a mainstay since the 1860s, continued to develop there, and settlers took up more areas along creeks where they raised cattle and some hay. To the north - in North Park - settlement was later; ranchers did not turn this land into cattle range until the 1880s. Hay was discovered a good local crop, and the area became a source of some of the world's finest hay. Mining continued on Independence Mountain, while around the turn of the century coal and copper were discovered in North Park. A small boom ensued, but nothing substantial came of it.

When the famous "Moffat Road" railroad came into Middle Park, then pushed on to Steamboat Springs, and later into Craig, transportation became cheap and easy. For the first time cattle and sheep could be shipped directly to Denver without long drives; and hay, coal, and wheat, along with other crops, could be easily exported and at a profit. The land was also opened to more and more settlers.

The hope was that the Yampa Coal Fields would provide the basic revenue for the Moffat Road; however, while a coal "boom" occurred in towns like Oak Creek, Phippsburg, Mount Harris, and others, the road was bankrupt by 1909. The promise of a railroad was never fulfilled.

Another "boom" during this period was oil. From its discovery in the White River country in the 1890s, to the massive exploitation of the mineral near Rangely in 1902 (Poole Well), oil was a marginal product. By 1920 the industry had developed to a point that numerous oil fields, such as the Moffat, Iles, Danforth, and other areas, were in full production. In North Park, the North McCallum field was also brought in during the mid-1920s.

Other post-1900 developments included the creation of Rocky Mountain National Park and Dinosaur National Monument. In 1920, the construction of U.S. Highway 40 provided the first paved road in northwest Colorado. These national parks and improved roads brought more tourists into northwestern Colorado, and railroads, auto/truck roads, and then airplanes, made the northwest more accessible.

In 1917 the last major homestead effort was made northwest of Craig. This was the Great Divide Homestead Colony Number One, developed by Volney T. Hoggatt and promoted by the Denver *Post*. Hundreds of settlers were lured into Great Divide where they scratched out a living dryland farming until the drought-filled days of the 1930s. This experiment in dry homesteading was a total failure, and was one of the last booms in the region.

A final "boom" occurred with the construction of the Moffat Tunnel, begun in 1923 and completed in 1927. With the completion of the tunnel, it was assumed that the Moffat Road would be finished into Salt Lake City, and the northwest would be saved. However, the Moffat Tunnel only shortened the railroad's route and, because of the miserable financial condition of the Moffat Road, the Denver and Rio Grande Western leased its right-of-way. By the 1930s the Dotsero Cutoff was completed and, for all practical purposes, Craig became a branch service line. The northwest again languished.

Since the 1930s, northwestern Colorado has subsisted on agriculture, oil, some coal, and more recently tourists, mostly skiers. Within the last ten years, oil shale development has shown promise. More importantly, due to the national energy demands of the last few years, the coal industry has revived and a new boom is imminent.

This region's history was one of constant "booms" that never worked out. From fur to mining, cattle to oil, coal to oil shale, and back to coal, the northwest corner of Colorado showed great promise, but for various reasons, it has never been able to fulfill the dream that seemed so real.

Chapter 1

NORTHWESTERN COLORADO

PRIOR TO EXPLOITATION

Northwestern Colorado includes an area extending west from the Continental Divide to the Utah-Colorado state line, and from north of Colorado (Grand) River basin to the Wyoming-Colorado line. Within this area lie a succession of wide valleys, several high mountain parks, and a series of major river drainages.

Farther west, Colorado is composed of broad floodplains on either side of major rivers, and within main drainages, smaller creeks and streams cut the landscape into massive buttes and narrow canyons. This region is watered by numerous subsidiary creeks running into the Yampa or Grand Rivers. One of the major features of the far northwestern corner is Brown's Park, extending sixty miles into Utah from Maybell, Colorado, on a northwesterly axis.

Major river drainages include the Colorado (Grand) River that begins at Grand Lake and is fed by the Fraser, Blue, and Eagle Rivers. North Park, one of the larger parks, is drained by the North Platte River and smaller streams such as the Michigan, Illinois, and Canadian. The Yampa Valley's major river is the Yampa (Bear), and it is fed by the Little Snake and Elk Rivers, as well as by smaller creeks such as Fortification. The White River Valley is watered by Piceance Creek, Douglas Creek, and other small perennial streams.

The area's climate is extreme. From the summer months when the temperature can exceed 100 degrees in the far northwestern corner, to the winter months in the mountain parks where the thermometer has recorded 54 degrees below zero, radical variations make agriculture and settlement difficult.[1] Generally, the mountain parks remain wet from May until July, while the lower areas are dry by late June. This climate plus the fluctuating seasonal water sources, mostly run-off from snowfall, make agriculture a limited and risky business.

To fully understand the geography of northwestern Colorado, it is important to know what geologic events transpired to modify the landscape. The base material upon which the area is built is Pre-Cambrian granite that was eroded into vast layers of flat sediment. These were then uplifted and re-eroded so that a series of sediments have been left over a period of millions of years.[2] Most of the sedimentation in the region and new beds of sandstone were laid down. Almost perfect fossil examples of early marine life can be found.[3]

Late in the Jurassic Period, Colorado was submerged. During this moist environment dinosaur bones that are found in Dinosaur National Monument were deposited. Plant and marine life provided fossil remains that became the coal and oil deposits that cover this region. During the Cretaceous Period the land was uplifted, with the Piceance and Axial Basins being created. Underlying these basins were the oil and coal deposits lift by organic matter buried in the region.[4]

The Tertiary Period of the Cenozoic Era saw a time of mountain building called the Laramide Orogeny. The Rocky Mountains, as we know them, were uplifted. The core of

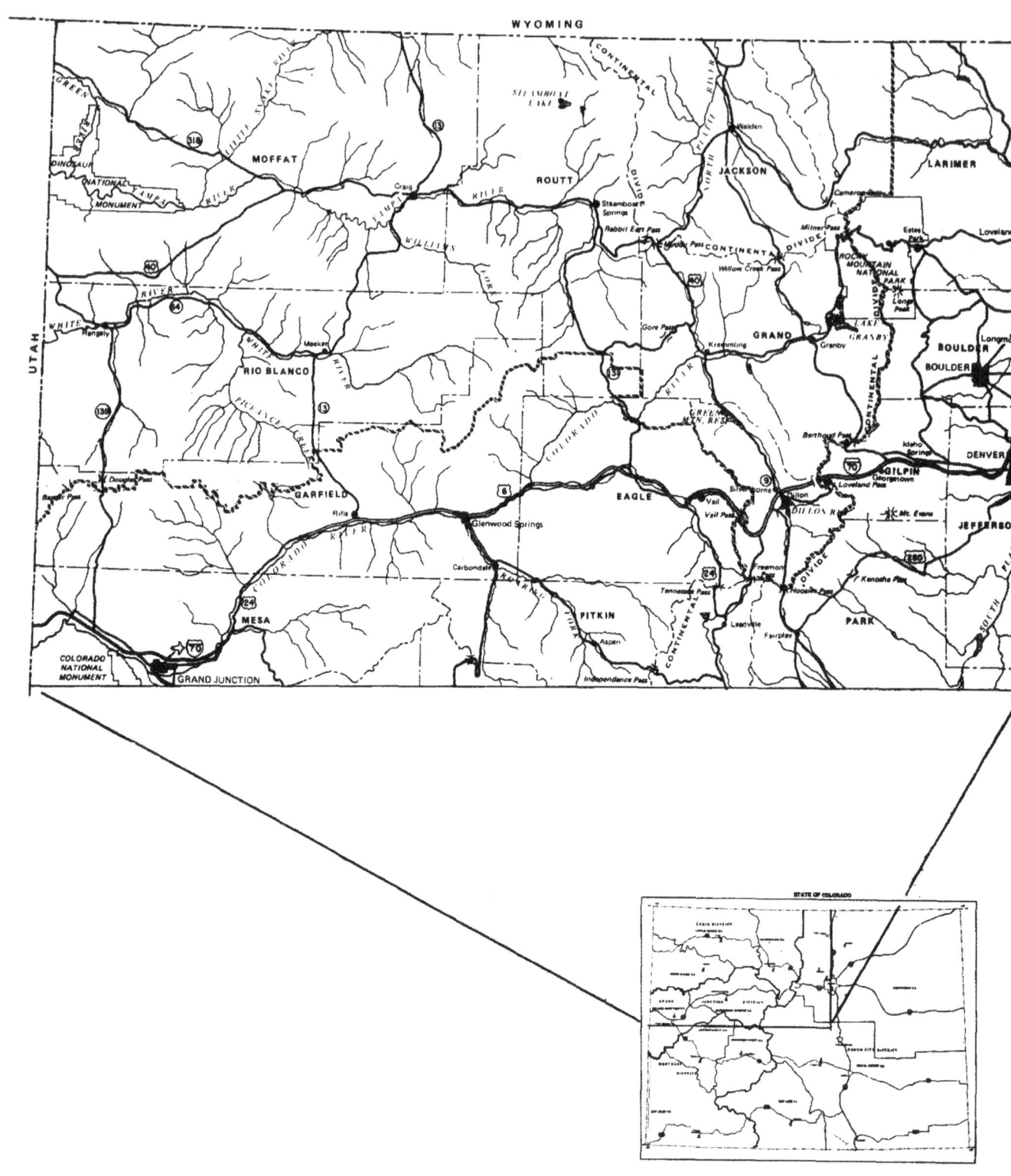

The Northwest Portion of Colorado, Outlining the Craig
District and Showing Geographic Features

12

the mountains was cracked and brought to the surface, where solutions of gold, silver, zinc, Lead, copper, and iron seeped into the fissures. This created the veins of gold and other minerals that are common in the Colorado Rockies. Localized deposits were also created by this building, including areas such as Hahns Peak and Independence Mountain. Additionally, an oily material called Kerogen was formed from the mud of Lake Uintah, that developed with the Laramie uplift, and from these deposits came the Green River formation of oil shales.

The final building period came in the Quaternary Period when the Ice Age descended on Colorado. During the Pleistocene Epoch, the state was selectively glaciated, and many of the features that we know today were created. To some extent the parks, Middle and North, were carved out, while mountains including the Rockies, the Park Range, and Elk Mountains were gouged out. Terminal moraines were dropped from glaciers and these formed dams across valleys; from these formations came lakes such as Grand Lake.[5]

Recent geologic events created the landforms that are currently known. These are a result of natural erosion by wind and water, along with geologic changes wrought by massive slides and other factors. Manmade features caused the most recent changes in the landscape. Such physical evidence as mines, foundations, road alignments, and other evidences are the more recent and possibly the most radical variations on the land since the Ice Age.

The advent of humans in the area is difficult to date. Man probably used the land for 10,000 years or more prior to the coming of Europeans. However, it is historic native Indians that are of interest as factors in settlement and development within the area. Prior to the Europeans, the northwest corner of the state was historically populated basically by three tribes of Indians. Of these groups, the largest was the Ute. The next most important tribe in the area was the Arapaho who, while plains natives, often used North and Middle Parks for summer hunting grounds. These lands were traditionally Ute domain, and conflicts often erupted over hunting rights. However, the Arapahos continued to use the near western areas despite Ute objections. The other tribe of consequence in the area was the Shoshoni, who were said to come into the Brown's Park area to winter. These people were probably the Wind River Shoshoni and are of the same linguistic group as the Ute. In this way they were able to exist with the Ute and there was rarely trouble between these peoples. Other tribes that had a minor impact on the area included the Cheyenne and to a lesser extent, the Navajo and Apache.

Within the Ute tribe there were subdivisions including Uncompahgre, Weeminuche, Muache, Capote, and others. These subdivisions related primarily to geographic locations and not major cultural differences. The Uncompahgre Ute were the main inhabitants of northwestern Colorado. These people were nomadic hunters who used the river valleys for shelter. They summered in high mountain parks stocked with abundant game, particularly elk, deer, and beaver, and when the weather turned cold they moved into the Yampa or White River valleys to spend their winter in comfort. The Ute were not known as hostile to Anglos at the time Europeans first described them. During the late seventeenth and early eighteenth centuries, the Ute were continually at war with the Arapaho, the Comanche, and other plains tribes. However, once the Uncompahgre moved into the mountainous interior, the constant warfare eased. They were friendly to Europeans and their only real enemies during the period of early Anglo-American occupation were the plains war parties and Arapaho who occasionally encroached Ute lands.

The Ute tended to live in small family groups scattered over wide areas, yet they retained a certain cohesion in times of trouble.[6] The Ute culture was changed radically by the introduction of the horse; once adapted, the horse was looked upon as a sacred animal. It was Ute wealth, and more valued, possibly, than a wife, children, or a dog.[7] Thanks to the horse which the Ute had by the 1680s, geographic ranges were considerably extended; due to new and better available food, the Ute advanced considerably in status among the natives of the West.[8] Eventually, Ute culture developed into a buckskin-horse-buffalo economy, with Plains Indians making a strong contribution to Ute materialism. The Ute expanded to the point that by the time Europeans came into their land, they ranged from Pike's Peak on the east to the Great Salt Lake on the west, and from Taos in the south, to Wyoming's Green River country on the north.[9]

The first recorded European visitors to northwestern Colorado were Spanish, in 1776. The Spanish were not new to the general area of Colorado; as early as 1695 Diego de Vargas, the reconquerer of New Mexico, had visited the San Luis Valley. Colorado was of little interest to the Spanish, however, for it showed no agricultural promise and precious minerals were not found. In 1765, Juan de Rivera was sent from Santa Fe to explore for minerals in Colorado. He reached the area of the Black Canyon of the Gunnison and also explored the San Juan region. Finding nothing of value, he returned home and reported that the area was of little worth. This ended Spanish interest in Colorado until 1776.[10]

In that year, the Spanish government in New Mexico decided to explore new routes to California from Santa Fe. The reason for the decision to go north was that the Hopi (Moqui) had blocked the most direct route across Arizona, and the Spanish, particularly the Church, were interested in establishing relations with the new California missions.[11] There was a trader's trail into Colorado that had been used since the Rivera expedition. It was upon this path that two Franciscan explorers led their small expedition. These men, Fray Silvestre Velez de Escalante and Fray Francisco Atanasio Dominguez, were determined to trace a new route into California. They projected that this could be done with minimum cost and without a large party.[12]

The governor at Santa Fe was interested in the project, and he willingly helped the two friars arrange their trip. Governor Pedro Fermin de Mendinueta provided material help and saw the expedition off on July 29, 1776. The little party of nine left Santa Fe and worked its way up to Abiquiu (New Mexico), from whence the group pushed northward into Colorado. By late August 1776, they were well into the present state of Colorado. They passed Dulce and then moved on to the San Juan River, past the Mesa Verde, and down to the Dolores River. [13]

From the Dolores, the party moved to the junction of Uncompahgre and Gunnison Rivers. They crossed the stream with the help of "Yuta" Indians. The party then moved north toward the White River. In doing so, they became the first Europeans to cross the Grand Hogback, the Grand River, and the Piceance Basin.

By September 5, 1776, the group reached the Debeque, Colorado area, from whence they trailed north along Roan Creek. The party left Roan Creek, traveled along the Roan Plateau and came to the headwaters of Douglas Creek. From here they proceeded through Douglas Canyon into the White River country. Along the way, they saw Canon Pintado (Painted Canyon) and what they thought were veins of gold along the canyon walls. [14] However, they made no attempt to mine. Upon emerging from Douglas Canyon, the group moved down the White River Valley into Utah. They camped at Jensen, Utah, on September 14, 1776, and then proceeded southwest across that state and into Arizona, finally returning to Santa Fe in late 1776 without having found a route to California. The knowledge gained from the expedition was not widely distributed and many of the areas explored for the first time remained "undiscovered." The Dominguez-Escalante expedition was of some value in that the resources of the Great Basin area were recorded. However, the Spanish were not interested in taking advantage of these discoveries; it was not for another forty years that Mexicans and Americans would venture far into this land.

NOTES FOR CHAPTER 1

1. Steven Payne. *Where the Rockies Ride Herd.* (Denver, Sage Books, 1965.), p. 244.

2. See: William W. Mallory, *Geologic Atlas of the Rocky Mountain Region,* (Denver, Rocky Mountain Association of Petroleum Geologists, 1972).

3. Linda L. Duchrow, "Geologic History of Colorado," (Denver, University of Colorado at Denver, 1974), Typescript, p. 8.

4. See: Nevin M. Fenneman, *The Yampa Coal Fields, Routt County, Colorado,* (Washington, D.C.: Government Printing Office, 1906).

5. See: Ferdinand V. Hayden, *United States Geologic Survey of the Territories, Annual Report, 1875,* (Washington, D.C.: Government Printing Office, 1875). Gustavus R. Beckler describes Middle Park's geology in this volume.

6. Marshall Sprague, *Massacre: The Tragedy at White River,* (Boston: Little Brown, 1957), p. 62.

7. Ibid, p. 63.

8. Warren L. d'Azevedo, et al. (eds.), *(The Current Status of Anthropological Research in the Great Basin; 1964.* (Reno: Desert Research Institute, 1966, p. 173.

9. Ibid, p. 178. See also: *James Grady, Environmental Factors in Archaeological Site Location, Piceance Basin, Colorado.* (Denver: Bureau of Land Management, 1980).

10. Herbert E. Bolton, *Pageant in the Wilderness,* (Salt Lake City: Utah State Historical Society, 1950), p. 6. Also: Angelico Chavez, (trans.), and Ted J. Warner (ed.), *The Dominguez-Escalante Journal,* (Provo, Utah: Brigham Young University Press, 1976).

11. Bolton, op, cit., p. 2.

12. Ibid., p. 9.

13. Frederic James Athearn, "Life and Society in Eighteenth Century New Mexico, 1692-1776," (Austin, Texas: University of Texas, 1974, Ph.d Dissertation), p. 245.

14. Bolton, op. cit., pp. 54-58.

Chapter 2

THE FUR TRADE

The fur trade in Colorado did not fully develop until the early 1820s, although some fur trappers were active in the area prior to that time. The Hudson's Bay Company continually worked the northern and central Rockies in addition to western Canada for nearly one hundred years after their charter was granted in the mid-1700s. The fur trade boomed during the early 1800s when European demand for pelts suddenly rose. In London, Berlin, Paris, Rome, and St. Petersburg, the need for furs for coats, robes, and hats increased dramatically. This caused North American fur seekers to expand their areas of trapping and trade.

At the same time, Americans came on the scene. In 1810 the upper Missouri River basin swarmed with American and British trappers. By 1808, the Yellowstone River country was trapped, and by 1810 the first American company was founded. Manuel Lisa, William Clark (of Lewis and Clark fame, and the Chouteau brothers of St. Louis founded the Missouri Fur Company that dominated the trade until 1814, when John Jacob Astor's American Fur Company surpassed it. The companies dealt mostly with private trappers who were scattered all over the west. By 1819 the northwest corner of Colorado was used by half-breed French trappers who worked for those that paid the best price.[1]

Several trappers were noted as being in the Green-Yampa (Bear) River areas of Colorado prior to 1822. Jean-Baptiste Chalifoux, otherwise known as Baptiste Brown, worked the area as early as 1820. He discovered the long valley of the Green that was subsequently named after him, Brown's Hole.[2] However, despite Baptiste Brown's knowledge of the area, there was little activity in the Hole. Possibly dispersed trappers used it for wintering purposes, but little else. Only twenty years later did Brown's Hole become a popular fur trade center. The only other early trapper known to be in the "Hole" was Maurice Le Duc, who claimed he came in 1819 or 1820.[3] Off and on, trappers made their way into the "Hole", but William H. Ashley opened the area on a large scale.

In 1822 "General" Ashley advertised in a St. Louis newspaper that he needed one hundred "enterprising young men" to form a trading party to exploit the Missouri River Basin. Before Ashley was finished, he had 180 recruits including most of the well-known trappers such as Jim Bridger, Thomas Fitzpatrick, Milton and William Sublette, Jedediah Smith, and many others. His first expedition up the Missouri River was a financial disaster and he quickly shifted operations to the Central Rockies. He sent Jedediah Smith and Thomas Fitzpatrick with a small party into the Rockies to test the beaver potential, and when Thomas Fitzpatrick returned to St. Louis in June, 1823, every pack horse was laden with fur. Ashley knew he had won.[4]

The Ashley party then set out in 1824 to develop this new area of the Rockies. In his journey of discovery, Ashley found his way across Wyoming down the Yampa Valley where he viewed Steamboat Springs, and noted Brown's Hole. From the Green River, he went north until he found a place for a rendezvous with his men;[5] the spot was called Pierre's Hole, along the Green River. Ashley decided that it was safer not to build permanent forts among the Indians, but rather to use a system of annual "rendezvous" that would assure a steady supply of furs ready for shipment back to St. Louis. In 1825, a caravan set out for that city and with it went Ashley, now a rich man. He and his partners sold out to Thomas Fitzpatrick, Milton Sublette, and Jim Bridger, who then formed the Rocky Mountain Fur Company in 1830.[6]

Naturally, the success of Ashley tempted others to try their luck in the field. In 1825, a party organized by Alexander Sinclair and Robert Bean moved into the North Park area to trap. They wintered at Brown's Hole and then returned to St. Louis.[7] This marked the first serious competition for the Rocky Mountain Fur Company in Colorado. From that year on, Brown's Hole became a regular stopping point for most fur trappers. With the coming of the Sinclair-Bean party, other men soon ventured into North, Middle and Brown's Parks. Antoine Robidoux visited Brown's Park in 1825, but chose to build a trading post in 1828 on the Gunnison River at its junction with the Uncompahgre. Later in the early 1830s, he built a fort in Utah near the later White Rocks Agency (see diagram, page 16a.), that he named Fort Uintah. It was also called Fort "Winty" or Fort Robidoux, and became a major trading post for the Yampa (Bear) River area. During his visits to the region, Robidoux also worked along the White River. His men were the first Europeans to work from Trappers Lake down the White River. The region was in use as early as 1824 or 1825 and continued to be a major fur source into the early 1840s. Robidoux and his men ranged from the Flattop Mountains to the Utah border and were likely the first American visitors to the Rangely, Colorado, country.

Other trappers also made their way into North Park, which was abundant with game. Thomas "Peg-Leg" Smith (so-called because he lost a leg when Milton Sublette was forced to amputate it due to gangrene), John Gantt, Christopher (Kit) Carson, Alexander Sinclair, and Calvin Jones were all known to frequent North and Middle Parks until the late 1830s.[8] Albert Gallatin Boone hunted in Middle Park as early as 1824-25. He moved to the Williams Fork River in the 1830s where he worked with William S. (Old Bill) Williams. Williams trapped the Bear River area as early as 1825.[9]

Fur Trapper and His Pony
Montana State Historical Society

While northwestern Colorado was extensively used for trapping purposes as early as 1825, Brown's Hole did not develop until the late 1830s. It was the construction of Fort Davy Crockett to service the fur trade in 1838 or 1839 that brought Brown's Hole to the forefront. Furs trapped in New Park (North Park) were often brought to Fort Crockett for trading. The Fort served as protection for trappers against the Indians who generally confined themselves to stealing horses. Many trappers also wintered in Brown's Hole.

By 1839, Fort Crockett was in full operation. The guiding lights behind the Fort were Prewett F. Sinclair, younger brother of Alexander Sinclair; Philip Thompson, and William Craig, who went into partnership in 1837 to try to buy and sell all furs in the area.[10] They were apparently successful, for most of the major figures in the fur trade appeared at Fort Crockett. In 1839 Kit Carson, Levin Mitchell, Bill New, Dick Owens, Joseph Walker, Tim Goodale, John Robertson (also called "Jack Robinson"), James Baker, Henry Fraeb (also called Frapp), Seth Ward, and Charles Kinney were known to visit Fort Crockett in 1839 and 1840.[11]

In addition to the regular fur trade customers who frequented Fort Crockett, there were visitors. A German, F. A. Wislizenus, discussed Fort Crockett in 1839 during a visit. He said of the fort: "It is a low one-story building constructed of wood and clay, with three connecting wings and no enclosure. Instead of cows, the fort had only some goats. In short, the whole establishment appeared somewhat poverty stricken, for which reason it is also known to the trappers by the name of Fort Misery."[12] Thomas Jefferson Farnham also saw the fort and had little good to say about it. Obadian Oakley and E. Willard Smith journeyed to the area and described the fort as being miserable in appearance.[13] When John Charles Fremont passed by the area in 1844, he found the fort abandoned with only a few walls standing.[14] By 1844, the fur trade was no longer profitable and Fort Crockett was abandoned. In 1866, all that remained of the site was an old building, a corral, and the ruins of some cobblestone chimneys. These ruins were located about two miles above the mouth of Vermillion Creek.[15]

Indians caused the fur trappers some moments of anxiety, but there were rarely fights over territorial incursions alone due to the fact that the trappers were trading with enemy tribes. However, in 1841, Henry Fraeb, a well-known fur man, along with Jim Baker and several dozen other trappers, were caught by a group of Cheyenne and Arapaho near Dixon, Wyoming, and battle ensued. Fraeb was killed while holing up his men in some rocks. Several Indians, outraged by the fur trappers' travels into Wyoming, killed Fraeb, wounded Baker, and injured a number of the other trappers. The traders escaped, but this battle became known as the largest single battle between Indians and fur trappers in Colorado history. The site was designated Battle Mountain and Battle Creek, while Fraeb was buried along Savery Creek.[16]

FORT ROBIDOUX

Length West Side	Length East Side	Width North End
50'-0"	50'-0"	50'-0"
39'-1-½"	39'-6"	24'-9"
89'-1-½"	89'-0"	74'-9"
1'-6"	1'-0"	1'-6"
90'-7-½"	90'-6"	76'-3"

Width South End		
50'-0"	76-½	
22'-0"	73-½	
72'-0"	1-½	
1'-6"	74 3-½=4	
73'-6"	(30)	

Manuscript of F. W. Cragin and Mr. J. M. Barker, September 3, 1902 Ft. Robidoux.

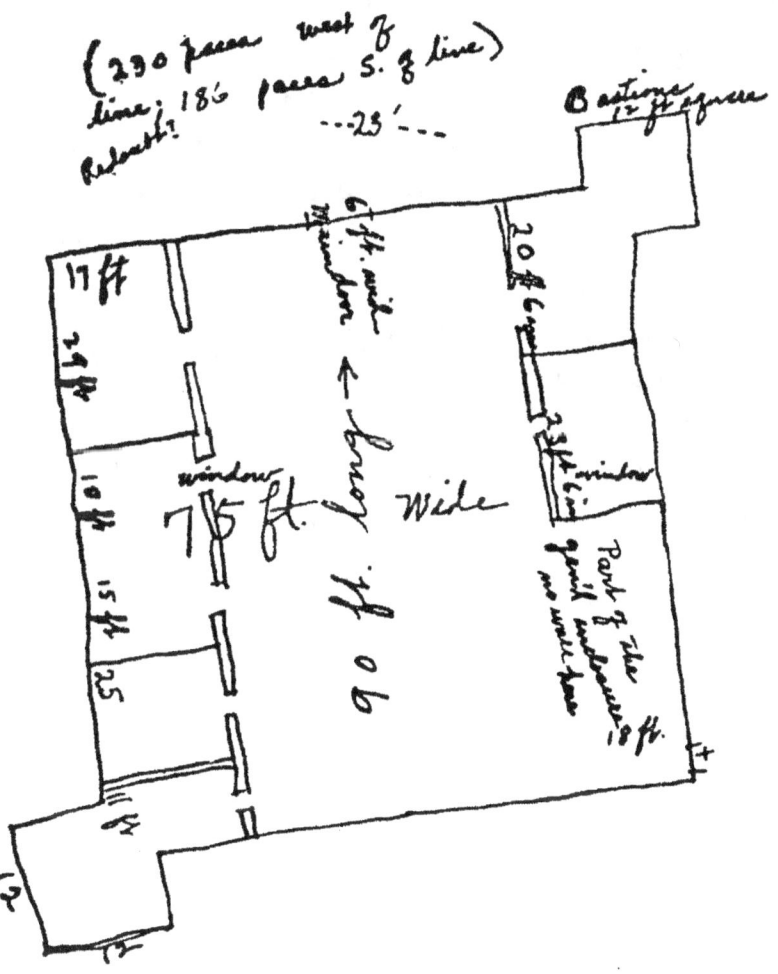

walls massive, of adobe:
(no sod on the valley
here; all clay-loam.
At x a dirt ridge runs
out east to theS. wall
and flush with it as if
a small tower or bastion
had fallen there; it's
only about 4 feet wide.

From: Original drawing in F. W. Cragin Manuscripts, Colorado Springs, Colo.

The main fur trade in northwest Colorado came to an end in the 1840's. There were two basic causes for the decline. The first, and most obvious was the lack of beaver pelts; most prime pelts had been trapped out. Second, a major change in fashion caused fur to lose popularity. The silk hat came into style in Europe, and soon fur pelt hats were no longer in demand.

In northwest Colorado there were a few trappers who refused to quit. Lory (Lowry) Simmons was trapping in Brown's Hole as late as the 1870's, while Gus Lankin was said to have been making his living trapping in Brown's Hole as late as 1878. He had a cabin located somewhere on Diamond Mountain, and was considered the last of the trappers.[17]

Other fur men found new employment. Jim Bridger, Charles Kinney, Bill Sublette, Jim Baker, Jack Robinson, and Tim Goodale all ran immigrant ferries on the Green River in Wyoming. Bridger sold his operation in 1859 and turned to scouting.[18] Tim Goodale was employed by Captain E. L. Berthoud in 1861 to guide him across the pass later named for the Captain, while Jim Baker was hired to guide Sir St. George Gore into North Park for his famous "hunt" of 1855.[19] He moved back along the Little Snake River in 1878 where he farmed until 1898, the year of his death; he was buried at Dixon, Wyoming.[20] Seth Ward left the fur trade, and through his connections became the post suttler at Fort Laramie, Wyoming. Here he made a fortune selling goods to the army, and died peacefully in 1903.[21] Kit Carson went on to become active in New Mexico in 1846, Carson was appointed Lieutenant-Governor.[22] Rufus B. Sage, who came to North Park in 1841, turned to a literary career and published his journals.[23]

Most of the fur trappers who were active in Colorado during the 1820's and 1830's had moved on by 1845. Many went south into New Mexico where a booming trade in furs was taking place. Some went into California where there were still opportunities in beaver, otter, and other pelts, not to mention a rich Mexican-American trade. The Colorado trappers took what they had come for, and then left when the resources were exhausted.

NOTES FOR CHAPTER 2

1. Ray A. Billington, *Westward Expansion,* (New York: Macmillan, 1974), pp. 379-389.

2. LeRoy R. Hafen (ed.), *The Mountain Men and the Fur Trade of the Far West,* (Glendale, California: Arthur H. Clark, 1966), VII, p. 57. (8 volumes).

3. F. W. Cragin Papers, Manuscripts, Pioneer Museum, Colorado Springs, Colorado, Notebook IV, p. 9.

4. David M. Frost, *Notes on General Ashley,* (Barre, Mass.: Barre Gazette, 1960), p. 12.

5. Dale L. Morgan (ed.), *The West of William H. Ashley,* (Denver: Old West Publishing Co., 1965), pp. 171-273.

6. Billington, op. cit., p. 385.

7. Hafen, Op. Cit., III, p. 340.

8. Hafen, Ibid., IV. p. 357; V. p. 197; VI. p. 208; IV, p. 301.

9. Hafen, Ibid., VIII, p. 34 and VIII, p. 34 and VIII, p. 373; VIII, p. 376.

10. Ibid., IV, p. 306.

11. Ibid., V, p. 241; V, p. 241; V, p. 284; V, p. 271; VII, pp. 152-153; VII, p. 250; III, pp. 137-139; III, p. 361; and IV, p. 264.

12. F.A. Wislizenus, *A Journey to the Rocky Mountains in the Year 1839,* (St. Louis: n.p., 1912), p. 129.

13. Hafen, op. cit., III, p. 341.

14. Ibid., IV, p. 309.

15. Cragin Papers, op. cit., unpaginated.

16. Hafen, op. cit., III, pp. 137-139.

17. Hafen, op. cit. VI, p. 322 and V, p. 322-323.

18. Cragin Papers, op. cit., Notebook V, p. 2, Notes 6 and 7.

19. Hafen, op. cit., VII, pp. 152-153; and Forbes Parkhill, *The Wildest of the West,* (Denver: Sage, 1957), pp. 133-134.

20. Hafen, op. cit.., III, p. 40 and III, p. 46.

21. Hafen, op. cit., III, p. 361.

22.   Chirstopher "Kit" Carson, *Autobiography,* (Chicago: Lakeside Press, 1935.)

23.   Rufus B. Sage, *His Letters and His Papers,* (Glendale, Calif: Arthur H. Clark, 1956).

Chapter 3

EXPLORATION

IN NORTHWESTERN COLORADO

Exploration by Americans in the far west began after Louisiana Territory was purchased by the United States in 1803. With this acquisition, millions of acres of unexplored land was added to the nation. In response series of expeditions and surveys were ordered by the government, beginning with Lewis and Clark, and not ending until 1876. The purpose of these survey efforts was to map the land and to provide basic information on the resources, native inhabitants, and flora and fauna of these vast new areas. Suitability for settlement was also to be determined. Usefulness of the land was uppermost in the minds of most Americans and for this reason, surveys were conducted at government expense and for public purposes. To insure that exploration of the west was accomplished, the United States government assigned the task to the U.S. Army. Within the Army, the Corps of Topographical Engineers were given the job of actual exploration.[1]

One of the first visitors to the northwest corner of Colorado included Captain Benjamin L. E. Bonneville, who explored the Great Basin in 1826, and then again in 1832, but this did little to improve knowledge of Colorado and Utah. Besides official government explorers, there were other travellers in the west.[2] Several parties interested in the west made long, hard treks into the wilderness. One such group was the Thomas Jefferson Farnham party of adventurers who took the Santa Fe Trail to Bent's Fort, from which they went northwest to the Blue River country, crossing the Continental Divide into Middle Park and then they moved west into the Yampa (Bear) Valley. Once on the Yampa, the party went on to Fort Davy Crockett in August of 1839, where Farnham described his stay. On the way to Crockett, the Farnham party observed Steamboat Springs, and crossed the country near the Little Snake River, that he noted was quite dry and useless. Brown's Park was described as a virtual paradise after the Little Snake.[3] Farnham noted that Brown's Park was rich and could be used for agriculture; he said that some vegetables were being grown there for the fort's consumption.[4] Upon leaving the fort, the party went up the Green River and then on to Oregon, their final destination.

In an area where there were few Europeans, Farnham and his group met a party led by F. A. Wislizenus of St. Louis. The two groups compared notes and then parted. Farnham's descriptions of Fort Crockett were glowing, while Wislizenus found it a miserable place. The two took different routes, and Wislizenus' was far easier; perhaps that is why he tended to be critical of the fort.[5]

Another private traveler, E. Willard Smith, visited Brown's Park in April 1840, and noted that Fort Crockett was still active. Smith also hunted in North Park, then he proceeded to the West Coast without providing much information about far western Colorado.[6]

In 1843, the first of two major army expeditions to map and survey the west began. John Charles Fremont was ordered to blaze trails into Oregon and California, and in general to discover practical routes for settlement in the west. To do this, Fremont was commissioned a second lieutenant in the Corps of Topographic Engineers. His second expedition of 1844 took him into Colorado.

Guided by Thomas "Broken Hand" Fitzpatrick, Fremont took a party from Fort St. Vrain in eastern Colorado to the Laramie Mountains by way of the Cache la Poudre River, and then from North Park into the Green River country along the Yampa Valley. Charles Preuss, the expedition's scientist, made observations of longitude, latitude, and took notes on the flora and fauna of the region.[7] The Fremont expedition stopped at Steamboat Springs, the name of which they gave the springs. The expedition then moved on to the Great Salt Lake in Utah.[8]

Upon reaching Salt Lake, the party turned around and marched back to the Uintah country, where they visited Antoine Robidoux at his fort (Fort Uintah), which was wiped out by Indians only a few weeks later.[9] From here Fremont moved into Brown's Hole, and found the remains of Fort Crockett. The group marched from Vermillion Creek, back to the St. Vrain region that took them back on to the Platte; from here they returned to St. Louis, using the Platte and Missouri River valleys.[10]

Fremont's observations of the country in western Colorado were typical. He found North Park and the Yampa Valley abundant in game. He saw little use for the lands west of the present Craig area, and he felt that Brown's Hole was of marginal value. He noted the continual outcroppings of coal, and he was interested in the numerous springs and mineral waters that were found in the region.[11] Other than these observations, the second Fremont expedition did little to improve knowledge of this region.

In 1845 Fremont was commissioned to further explore Colorado in preparation for possible war with Mexico. Relations between the United States and Mexico were poor since the proposed annexation of Texas in 1844. Some popular sentiment in the nation demanded war. The Army was aware of this and tried to prepare; they needed routes for invasion and sent out Fremont to find appropriate pathways. His third expedition was for military purposes only.

This adventure was guided by Kit Carson, and took Fremont up the Arkansas River to Tennessee Pass over which his party crossed into the Grand (Colorado) River Valley. They then turned north and reached the White River. From here they marched west along the White until it joined the Green River. From the Green, they moved west across Utah and Nevada into California. Fremont's journals make little mention of Colorado; this was understandable in that there was no interest in science on this trip. The area was crudely mapped and then forgotten; California was of more concern.[12]

Fremont's contribution of knowledge of the west cannot be underestimated; through his mapping and descriptions of the land, the public and the government learned what was there. Western Colorado was written off as "worthless." A major event in the region was needed to create interest.

The stimulus came in 1859 with the discovery of gold along Cherry Creek near Denver. The Russell Brothers of Georgia found a little of the precious metal in placers along this waterway, and through continual "booming" by eastern and mid-western newspapers, a gold rush began to Colorado. The Pikes Peak Boom brought an estimated 100,000 people into Colorado. Soon it was evident that "free" gold along the creeks was not sustaining. As miners worked their way up the various creeks along the Front Range, Clear Creek proved the best. By 1861, the towns of Central City, Georgetown, and Empire were booming mining camps, and settlement was proposed in Middle Park. William Byers, editor and owner of the *Rocky Mountain News*, bought Hot Sulphur Springs in 1861, and planned to turn it into a tourist resort. However, before that could happen an access road was needed. [13]

At Byers urging, the citizens of Empire decided it wise to provide a road into Middle Park. A Swiss engineer named Edward L. Berthoud was hired to blaze a trail over the mountains. Guided by ex-trapper Tim Goodale, Berthoud and his party left Empire May 10, 1861, and traced a route over a logical pass through the Rockies. It took the group seventeen days to cross the Divide. [14] They concluded that this route would require 111-1/2 miles of roadway from Golden City (Golden, Colorado) to Hot Sulphur Springs. The cost was projected at $18,040; Berthoud concluded that such a road was possible. [15] However, due to a singular lack of traffic into Middle Park, the wagon road actually built was barely passable, and rarely used. Byers was unable to stir interest, and not until the 1870s did a new and better road come to life. Berthoud's expedition was important in providing a passage over the Divide, thus opening Middle Park.

Berthoud later blazed a proposed rail route across western Colorado, following the White River and then the Green on to Salt Lake. Jim Bridger was his guide, but nothing came of these efforts. The Army was called in to provide railway surveys during the 1850s, and John W. Gunnison surveyed Colorado to provide information about the Gunnison River country. This was the last official effort until the late 1860s when a new survey was made in northwestern Colorado.

John Wesley Powell was chosen for the job of surveying the White River country, northwestern Colorado, and the Green River. This awesome task began in 1868 when Powell started his preliminary work. He gathered a party of men at Fort Bridger, Wyoming, and then he marched them down to the White River. Here, near the present site of Meeker, Colorado, in a small park, his party wintered. Powell Park was just west of the White River

Indian Agency founded in 1868.[16]

Powell, having successfully spent the winter in Powell Park, prepared to leave in the spring of 1869. His plan was to survey the Green River, stopping to take latitude and longitude readings, in addition to providing basic mapping for the area. This rugged river had never been fully explored although some fur trappers including Jim Bridger claimed they had boated part-way down the Green. Powell's crew included nine men in three specially designed wooden boats. By the time the party reached the junction of the Green and Yampa Rivers, they had lost one boat and considerable quantities of supplies. They passed through the Flaming Gorge and into the Canyon of Ladore (Brown's Hole). Powell's men continued down the Green River to the Grand River, where they went into the Grand Canyon, reaching Collville, Utah, during the summer of 1869.[17]

The Powell survey of 1869 provided new and more accurate information on northwestern Colorado. The area was described by Powell as being of marginal quality for agriculture, and he concluded that the only way to make it useable was to irrigate on a massive basis.[18] However, Powell noted that there was not enough water readily available for such efforts. Powell's insight that the arid west would require irrigation went unnoticed until the late 1880s when water diversion projects became not only standard, but almost fashionable. Powell realized that water was the key to survival in the west, but equally he noted that the land was simply not suited to this sort of abuse. In later years, many dry-land farmers would regret the government's not heeding Powell's warnings.[19]

He described Brown's Park: "...natural meadow lands are found interspersed with the fine groves of cottonwood." He also noted that: "Some of the bench lands are well adapted to irrigation, but a portion of them and the foothills back of them are naked, valueless bad lands."[20] He estimated there were only ten square miles of irrigable land in Brown's Park.[21]

The Powell survey included valuable information on the condition of lands in the far west. Powell felt that this land was indeed not suited for agriculture, and he did not see it as cattle land. Nonetheless, Powell's main objective of tracing the Green and Grand (Colorado) Rivers was achieved, and it would be up to others to finish exploration in western Colorado.

NOTES FOR CHAPTER 3

1. See: William H. Goetzmann, *Army Exploration in the American West, 1803-1863,* (New Haven: Yale University Press, 1959) and William H. Goetzmann, *Exploration and Empire,* (New York: Knopf, 1966).

2. LeRoy R. Hafen, *Colorado and Its People,* (New York: Lewis, 1948), p. 89.

3. Reuben G. Thwaites, *Travels in the Far West,* (Cleveland: A.W. Clark, 1906), 2 Vols., p. 244 and p. 251.

4. Ibid., p. 252.

5. Wislizenus, op. cit., p. 129.

6. LeRoy R. Hafen, "With Fur Traders in Colorado: 1839-1840: The Journal of E. Willard Smith," *Colorado Magazine,* Vol. 27, No. 3, July, 1950, pp. 161-188.

7. Goetzmann, *Army,* op. cit., pp. 86-87. See also: Donald Jackson and Mary Lee Spence, *The Expeditions of John Charles Fremont,* (Urbana: University of Illinois Press, 1970), 2 Vols.

8. Jackson and Spence, op. cit., p. 477.

9. Goetzmann, *Army,* op. cit., p. 101.

10. Ibid., pp. 101-103.

11. Jackson and Spence, op. cit., p. 470. See also: Allan Nevins (ed), *Narratives of Exploration and Adventure* by John Charles Fremont, (New York: Longmans, Green, 1956).

12. Goetzmann, op. cit., p. 119.

13. Louise C. Harrison, *Empire and the Berthoud Pass,* (Denver: Big Mountain Press, 1964), p. 203.

14. Ibid., pp. 56-61.

15. Ibid., p. 60.

16. Richard Bartlett, *Great Surveys of the American West,* (Norman: University of Oklahoma, 1962), p. 235.

17. Goetzmann, *Exploration,* op. cit., p. 517. The boats were named: *Kitty Clyde's Sister, Maid of the River* and *The Emma Dean.*

18. John W. Powell, *U.S. Public Lands Commission,* (Washington: Government Printing Office, 1879), pp. 160-165.

19. Ibid., pp. 17-19. See also; Donald Worster, *The Dust Bowl* (New York: Oxford University Press, 1979), for a modern discussion of Powell's environmental ideas.

20. Ibid., p. 16.

21. Ibid., p. 164.

Chapter 4

MINING AND TRANSPORTATION

IN EARLY WESTERN COLORADO

Gold! The magic mineral that brought thousands of fortune seekers to Colorado promoted this state's first boom. As miners worked their way up the canyons and gullies, they discovered "free" gold in placers. This meant that along watercourses, flakes and bits of gold were abundant and could be panned or sluiced. However, major sources of gold were locked in hardrock quartzite that required expensive milling. Hence, early miners confined themselves to creeks and rivers.

As the surge of civilization swept against the Rockies, miners passed over the Divide and found that the Blue and Eagle River valleys were rich in gold placers. In 1859, the first major mining town on the western slope was founded. This was Breckenridge, named after John C. Breckinridge of Kentucky, a leading American politician. However, his name was somehow misspelled and the incorrect spelling has persisted.[1] By 1860 various gulches along the Blue River were under placer mining while a few hard rock shafts were sunk. In 1861 the population of the district was over 5,000, and other mining towns soon arose.[2]

During the early 1860s, hundreds of men fanned out over the Colorado Rockies, filtering into the parks, and then working to the far west. Among these men were Joseph Hahn, a German immigrant, William Doyle and George Way. Hahn wandered into the Elk River area in the early 1860s and discovered placer gold; he was unable to develop his discovery until after the Civil War.[3] In 1865 he took in Way and Doyle as partners, and the little group moved to Hahn's Peak. Doyle reported: "We found gold on every side of the peak, but not in sufficient quantities to pay for work with the pan, which was the only means we had of washing it out."[4] When fall, 1865 came, the men quit for the winter. In 1866, they guided some fifty men back to Hahn's Peak and began serious mining operations. They found the rich yields running from ten to fifteen dollars per shovelful, and a boom began.[5] Shortly after July 1866, a mining district was organized and Hahn was elected "surveyor" Doyle "recorder," and Way "judge."[6]

With winter approaching, the men agreed to split up. Doyle and Hahn were to remain at camp while Way went out for various supplies, including saws to build sluice boxes. Way failed to return, and soon Hahn and Doyle were on the verge of starvation. In April 1867 the two men set out seeking help. On the way to Empire, using snowshoes, Hahn died of exposure, and Doyle was found nearly dead at Troublesome Creek in Middle Park.[7] George Way, never heard from again, was accused of running off with the money that was entrusted him to buy goods. The upshot of the Hahn affair was that Hahn's Peak was forgotten.

Hahn's Peak was "rediscovered" in 1867 or 1868 by accident. A local resident known as "Bibleback" Brown (so-called because of his humped back), and whose actual name was John Brockmeyer, found some rusting mining tools along Willow Creek in the Hahn's Peak

Slater and Brown built a cabin along Savery Creek and began mining operations. The news of the strike reached Rawlins, Wyoming, and in 1872 the first family in the Elk River Valley moved in to stay. Noah Reader and his family were helped by Slater and Brown to construct a cabin, and settlement in the valley had begun.[8]

In 1872, the same time the upper Elk River was occupied, Hahn's Peak became a booming mining town. Its population increased to over 500 during the summers, but the region was deserted during the winters. The citizens of Hahn's Peak felt secure enough to create a mining district in 1874. At this time officials were elected, and the boundaries of the district were defined as being the Bear (Yampa) River to five miles the other side of Hahn's Peak and from the Little Snake River to five miles east of Hahn's Peak.[9] In 1876 this district was carved from Grand Bounty, and Hahn's Peak, being the largest town in the area at the time, became county seat of Routt County.

Hydraulic Mining, 1888
Montana State Historical Society

As was typical of mining areas, the Hahn's Peak District had numerous smaller camps. Such places as Columbine, Farwell (National City), Whiskey Park, and Slavonia were built in and around Hahn's Peak. These towns were purely summer camps and were used as bases for localized placer mining. Poverty Bar, Bugtown, and other small places provided camps a bit rougher than "civilized" towns like Hahn's Peak. First mining was placer, using pans and sluice boxes. By the 1880s major hydraulic mining enterprises took over and proceeded to wash away hillsides; this was vastly more profitable but hard on the landscape. It was estimated that some fifty miles of ditches were built to carry water for hydraulic purposes. Additionally, most of the smaller mining companies turned to the use of hydraulic equipment, some of which can still be seen at the townsite of Hahn's Peak.[10]

Agriculture developed by 1867 near the mining district. S. B. Reid was growing vegetables in that year, while the Elk River Valley saw an introduction of cattle by the mid-1870s. The primary population center of northwestern Colorado was Hahn's Peak, until nearly 1875. At that time, new settlers arrived and began to use the Yampa River Valley.[11]

Closer to the mountains, the other major mining district in the northwest sector was Breckenridge District, which flourished during the 1870s and 1880s. By the mid-70s, some eighty-four miles of ditches were built from the Blue River so as to provide water power for sluice and hydraulic mining.[12]

William Blackmore noted in 1869 that the Blue River country was producing silver ore averaging $600 per ton, and that copper had been discovered in Middle Park near Conger Mesa. He predicted a boom in that region but it never came. He stated that northwestern Colorado, as yet, showed few signs of development in that "No lodgement amounting to permanent occupation has yet surmounted the rigors of the Sierra and found a location within this area."[13]

The other area of early mining activity in northwestern Colorado was in North Park. By the early 1870s Independence Mountain was under production. These were placer claims, and there were several major operations going by 1875. From the Rabbit Ears Range north to Wyoming, scattered placer sites were worked. The Endomile claim was 1500 feet by 300 feet and showed $20 to $35 per ton in gold.[14] The largest mine was the Mitchell Placer operation; that was 160 acres in size and had 135 feet of flumes, 100 feet of pits, and one shaft. Production was estimated at three dollars per day per man. Gold was the primary mineral extracted.[15] Lead, copper, and zinc also were produced. These two placers, discovered in 1875, were worked off-and-on until the turn of the century.

A major problem that faced western Colorado during the 1860s and 1870s was the total lack of easy transportation. Even Breckenridge was not served by a railroad until 1882 when the Denver, South Park, and Pacific (DSP & P) Railroad reached that town.

The United States long projected transcontinental rail routes, but the Civil War intervened and prevented development of a main line. However, after the war, interest was renewed and construction began on a national railroad. From the east, the Union Pacific Railroad built westward out of Omaha, while to the west, the Central Pacific started to build over the Sierras to meet the oncoming Union Pacific. A railroad was uppermost in the minds of westerners, and businessmen in Denver attempted to get the Union Pacific to build to Denver and through the Rockies. The town of Empire went to work trying to convince the railroad that Berthoud Pass was an ideal route. Captain E. L. Berthoud was called in to consult with the railroad. He advised a narrow gauge route over the pass. It was estimated that the cost of construction would come to $100,000 per mile.[16]

William Byers in his *Rocky Mountain News*, urged the citizens of Empire to complete the wagon road over Berthoud Pass so the Union Pacific engineers could see the route in its "best light."[17]

Needless to say, Byers had an interest in the plan for the railroad would pass by Hot Sulphur Springs. It was projected that by using the Berthoud Pass route, 209 miles could be saved compared to the Wyoming route, equally $178,920 in costs could be cut. However, nobody thought to mention the cost of maintenance during winter.[18] In the end, the Union Pacific used the southern Wyoming route and by-passed Colorado.

When the Union Pacific reached Rawlins, Wyoming, transportation south into northwest Colorado became possible. By 1868 the only roads into northwest Colorado led out of Wyoming into places like Hahn's Peak. The railroad helped bring in settlers, and by the mid-1870s there were homesteads scattered along the Yampa River Valley. In 1873, a weekly mail route from the Little Snake River to Rawlins was begun under the auspices of R. M. Dixon. The Dixon Post Office (now Dixon, Wyoming) was the first to serve northwestern Colorado. It took care of Hahn's Peak, the Yampa Valley, and the Elk River Valley.[19]

The railroad also brought visitors to the area. In 1869, English adventurer Frederick T. Townshend came to Laramie by rail and then visited North Park. He described a hunting trip out of Fort Sanders, Wyoming (Laramie). Townshend stated that North Park was "... a plain about thirty miles long by fifteen broad through which flows the Platte River, rising in one of the surrounding mountains."[20] The party, including some soldiers, were attacked by unspecified Indians (probably Ute) but the natives were driven off without casualties. The Townshend trip indicated that the transcontinental railroad made access to northwestern Colorado easier.[21]

Thanks to having a rail line within fifty miles of the northwestern corner of Colorado, the Yampa (Bear), Little Snake, Elk, and White River Valleys were available for development. By the 1870s cattle were brought into the region, both because of good grasses and cheap transportation. North and Middle Parks also benefited from the Union Pacific on the same basis.

NOTES FOR CHAPTER 4

1. Mark Fiester, *Blasted, Beloved Breckenridge,* (Boulder: Pruett Press, 1973), p. 16.

2. Ibid., pp. 151-157.

3. John Rolfe Burroughs, *Where the Old West Stayed Young,* (New York: Morrow, 1962), p. 90.

4. Ibid., as quoted in Burroughs, p. 91.

5. Ibid., p. 91.

6. Ibid., p. 91.

7. Ibid., pp. 92-93. See also: Charles Leckenby, "Discovery of Gold at Hahn's Peak and the Tragic Death of Joseph Hahn" in *Tread of Pioneers,* (Steamboat Springs, Colorado: Steamboat *Pilot,* 1944) and Thelma V. Stevenson, *Historic Hahn's Peak.*

8. Burroughs, op. cit., pp. 94-95.

9. Ibid., p. 97.

10. Wilbur F. Stone, *History of Colorado,* (Denver: S.L. Clarke, 1918), 4 Vols. I, p. 298.

11. *CWA Interviews,* Routt County, Colorado, 1933-34, Typescript, S.B. Reid Interview.

12. William Blackmore, *Colorado, Its Resources and Prospects,* (n. l., n.p., 1869), pp. 134-135.

13. Ibid., p. 21, p. 38 and p. 77.

14. Robert A. Corregan and David F. Livgane, *Colorado Mining Directory,* (Denver: Colorado Mining Directory Co., 1883), p. 314.

15. Ibid., p. 315.

16. Harrison, op. cit., p. 203.

17. Ibid., p. 203.

18. Ibid., pp. 214-215.

19. Burroughs, op. cit., p. 100.

20. Frederick T. Townshend, *10,000 Miles of Travel, Sport, and Adventure,* (London: n.p., 1869), pp. 155-156.

21. Ibid., p. 157.

Chapter 5

CONFRONTATIONS:

SETTLEMENT VERSUS THE UTE INDIANS

When the Ute nation moved into the White River Valley, millions of acres of virgin lands were lost to European settlement. To most Americans during the nineteenth century, and especially to Coloradans, such a potential loss of production was nearly sinful. To the mind of the 19th-century American, land was for one purpose: it was to be used to produce for profit. Whether by mineral exploitation, timber cutting, or agriculture, each acre of land had to return on the investment, no matter how poor the quality of land involved. Most Americans had no concept of the marginal lands that lay west of the Rockies; to them all acreage was fertile and productive. This simply was not true for the vast tracts of northwestern Colorado. Only the river valleys where water could be diverted were at all usable. Yet, the 19th-century mind saw millions of acres of land going to waste, in the hands of indolent Indians who would rather hunt than farm.

To the average 19th-century American, the Indian was a creature to be pitied. He was clearly a being that needed to be Christianized, as most religious leaders so informed the public; he needed to be taught to read and write; but most of all he needed to become a self-sufficient farmer. The prevailing theory was that the Indian was to be sedentary, taught skills, educated, and then he could become a productive citizen. The public was told that the American Indian was to be civilized, meaning that he must become a white man and adopt a value system entirely different from his own.

For the Indian, the task was nearly impossible. For hundreds of years most western American Indians were nomadic - hunting in the summers, wintering in warm valleys. Now they were told to move into houses, live in one place year round, and farm the land. This concept was totally alien to the Indian. Indians did not want to accept the demands of the white man. He was willing to make concessions such as wearing white man's clothes, eating his food, and even praying to his God, but to till the soil was asking too much.[1]

In this context, the Utes were forced to accept an Indian agency that was designed for "conversion." The agents were religious men, ministers, who it was assumed, knew what the Indian needed in terms of redemption. It was into this cultural conflict that Nathan Meeker maneuvered himself. He was a typical 19th-century American who believed in all the prevailing principles of Indian welfare. The Utes, at first, gracefully accepted and tolerated him, but he demanded too much too fast, and the changes that were required by him proved overly demanding for the Ute people.

The first movements of Europeans across the mountains were small enough that the

47

Utes did not worry about losing their hunting lands. But, by the late 1860s and the early 1870s, scattered settlers came into prime Ute lands. In addition, minerals were discovered in the San Juan Mountains. Lodes were believed to be large and profitable. By 1870, many western settlers were demanding access to these rich lands. However, there was one major problem: the lands in question belonged to the Ute tribes. Citizens of Denver, including most leading businessmen, demanded the natives be removed and that the San Juans be opened for settlement. Some more radical members of the community demanded extermination.[2]

In 1873, the Ute problem in southern Colorado was ameliorated when a treaty was negotiated by Felix Brunot by which the Utes gave up all claims to the San Juan Mountains. In return, the Utes agreed to move to two agencies: one on Los Pinos Creek in Southern Colorado, one along the White River in western Colorado. The Brunot Treaty provided a temporary answer to a sticky problem and, thanks to the annuities, a promise of land, and an influential, progressive chief, Ouray, the Utes were peacefully relocated.[3]

Luckily, the people of Colorado were able to deal with an intelligent and perceptive Ute chief who saw that resistance would do no good. Ouray, who spoke English and Spanish and who was wise enough to realize that no one could stop European progress, used his powers to persuade his tribes to accept their fate. In doing so, he prevented years of bloodshed that could have otherwise occurred.

While the Treaty of 1873 allowed Anglo settlement in the San Juans, many settlers who moved illegally into Middle and North Parks resented the use of the area by the Utes for hunting. It was claimed the Indians started forest fires, ran off livestock, and wantonly killed animals.[4]

The Ute move into White River Agency was peaceful and organized. Here Utes could hunt, fish, and live as they always had. In addition, they were granted an annuity of some $10,000 that provided food, clothing, and other goods. The problem came when agents tried to force the Utes to "learn white ways."[5] The Brunot Treaty granted all lands from the Continental Divide west into Utah and from the White River north to Wyoming to the Ute nation. This meant that the Utes were given choice hunting grounds, as well as excellent agricultural lands. However, the Ute saw no reason why they should not continue to use all hunting land in the old traditional manner. The United States government saw the question in a different light. Secretary of the Interior's Carl Schurz Indian policy called for the "civilization" of the natives of America. This meant that Indians should be taught English, they should learn to read and write, they should become agriculturally oriented, and they should wear European clothing and live in his type of houses. In short, they were to be transformed from nomads into a sedentary people; to become carbon-copy white men. That this policy was common was in evidence no more strongly than at White River.

The White River Agency had a history of problems. Since its establishment in 1868, the agency had seen several agents come and go. Most left in total frustration. The next to last agent, Reverend H. E. Danforth, quit because the government failed to deliver promised annuities on schedule. The Utes deeply resented the fact that goods such as flour, blankets, and other supplies sat in depots at Rawlins, Wyoming, and rotted.[6]

To succeed Danforth, Nathan Cook Meeker was chosen. In many respects he was the worst possible choice, while in other ways he was perfect - a visionary altruist. Meeker, a founder of Greeley, Colorado (the Union Colony), and a minister, was also a skilled agriculturalist. Meeker was sixty-seven years old and in deep financial trouble when he gained the appointment to the White River Agency. He was given the job, thanks to political pull, by Carl Schurz. Meeker saw his position as an opportunity for testing out theories on Indian recivilization, while the job also would help pay off debts incurred at Greeley.

In 1878, Meeker moved to the White River Agency, which was then located just east of present-day Meeker. He quickly surveyed the region and decided to move the agency downriver to Powell Park, which he felt was perfect for agriculture. He planned to irrigate the lowlands using the White River, to build the Utes houses, to provide a school, to put up a commissary that would dole out annuities, and to fence the land in the fashion of European agriculture. These concepts were totally new to the Ute, who while interested, failed to understand.[7]

Upon arriving at White River, Meeker met several Ute chiefs, including Douglas (so-called because he looked like Steven A. Douglas), Jack or Captain Jack, who had been raised by a Mormon family, the medicine man Johnson, and the fat Colorow. Douglas was the main spokesman for the Utes, and when Meeker explained his great plans, Douglas said that the tribe was not interested. When Meeker said that these plans were orders from Washington, D.C., the Utes, awed by "Washington," agreed to try the new system.[8]

With Douglas' and the other Utes' reluctant approval, Meeker began his experiment. The agent began by moving the agency to Powell Park, where he erected several buildings, including a house for himself, a school, and a store. His daughter, Josephine, was on the government payroll as schoolmistress and doctor. His wife, Arvella, became the self-appointed religious teacher of the natives.[9] Meeker found that his main problem was keeping the Utes on the reservation. They were constantly moving around to hunt. They naturally needed guns and ammunition, for which they traded goods with merchants at Hayden and Windsor (later Craig), Colorado. Meeker decided this "impeded progress" and planned to keep the Indians on the reservation by using their rations as bait.

Meeker imported his employees from Greeley, where he knew "sober, upright men" to work with the Indians. He employed a Mr. Curtis from the Los Pinos Agency to supervise the work of ditch digging, which began under his and Captain Jack's auspices. Over 5,000 feet of irrigation ditches were built; the Indians were paid and everyone settled in peaceably for the winter of 1878.[10] Through the summer of 1879, Meeker worked with the Utes trying to get them interested in crops that could pay for the agency. Meeker found the Indians became more and more disinterested; soon most had left for the mountains to hunt. Meeker's letters progressed from optimistic in March 1878 when he first arrived, to more and more gloomy. By September 1879, his communications showed fear, not just despair.[11]

During the summer of 1879, Meeker's plan seemed to go fairly well. However, there were several incidents that increased tensions. First, a series of forest fires swept the Parks and much of the Yampa Valley; it was an extremely dry summer and such fires were natural. However, many European settlers in the various Parks, especially Egeria Park, blamed the Utes, claiming they were trying to get rid of settlers by burning them out. The fires caused such an uproar that numerous complaints poured into Denver, and the governor's office asked for troops. Indeed, some forty troops were sent to Middle Park from the 9th Cavalry Regiment located in the San Luis Valley. These were the "Buffalo Soldiers," an all-black regiment, much feared and hated by the Utes.[12] The other incident that summer was the reported burning of a home near Hayden in August 1879. A "posse" from Hot Sulphur Springs was sent to capture the two Indians considered responsible for the "outrage," "Bennett" and "Chinaman." They were found. Meeker, having been apprised of the situation, refused to go to Hayden to look at the home. Douglas said it was not touched, which was true. Meeker said that if a white man said that it was burned, then Douglas lied.[13]

As summer progressed, Meeker was eager to get as much land as possible under cultivation. He decided that a racetrack the Indians used at the agency had to go, because the field should be put to productive use; racing was wasting the time of the natives; there were too many horses for the park, and there was continual gambling. When Meeker suggested the Indians should kill some of their animals to lessen the grazing burden on Powell Park, the Utes were outraged.[14]

On September 10, 1879, tensions that were growing came to a head. Chief Johnson went to Meeker's home to discuss the horse track's destruction. Meeker refused to listen to Johnson's protestations and the chief, in anger, shoved Meeker against a hitching post. The old man fell and bruised himself. This "assault" caused Meeker to wire Rawlins, Wyoming, with the message that he was seriously injured by Johnson, and that a plowman had been shot at on September 8.[15] He also requested help from either Governor Frederick Pitkin or General John Pope. Neither the War Department nor the Bureau of Indian Affairs felt it necessary to send troops at that point.

Finally, after much communication between Nathan Meeker; Fort Fred Steele, Wyoming; General Pope; and the War Department, it was decided to send troops to White River to arrest the troublemakers and to restore order. In late September, Major Thomas T. Thornburgh was ordered to march to White River with a detachment of 190 men. He had with him two companies of cavalry under the commands of Captain J. S. Payne and Lieutenant B. D. Price, and a long supply train.[16] They camped along Fortification Creek, at the mouth of Blue Gravel Creek, and then marched to the Yampa River where a depot was established just south of Lay, Colorado. Thornburgh, totally unaware of conditions at White River, was forced to rely on his scouts, including Joe Rankin, an avid Indian-hater.

On the second day out, the Thornburgh detachment camped along the Bear (Yampa) River, and then moved into Coal Creek Canyon not far from White River. Here they met Douglas and Colorow, along with Captain Jack. Major Thornburgh and the natives talked about what the soldiers were doing in the area, and Thornburgh explained he was ordered there by Washington. Rankin did his best to discredit the Ute's claims that the Utes came in peace and would leave the soldiers alone if the troops did not come to White River. Thornburgh, much to his credit, ignored Rankin. Thornburgh promised that he would reconsider moving to the agency and that he would tell Douglas what he decided before he marched.

Meeker, in the meantime, sent a message to Thornburgh. He asked that five men be sent to the agency to look over the situation, and that Thornburgh camp nearby.[17] Thornburgh replied that he would set up a base along the Milk River, and then send five men with E. H. Eskridge (an agency employee) to White River.[18] Meeker wrote to Thornburgh on September 29 that he was expecting the five men the next day, and that Douglas would fly the American Flag as a sign of peace; the letter never reached Thornburgh.

In order to reach White River, Thornburgh had to traverse a small canyon opening into the valley. Here, as Rankin pointed out, would be a perfect place for an ambush. This was where the Utes, under Douglas, waited along the canyon rims, anxious to see what would happen. At this point, Douglas and Colorow lost control of the young warriors. Douglas and Thornburgh both expected to talk, but someone opened fire, and before Douglas could stop the shooting, the Utes and the U.S. Army were engaged in battle.

Thornburgh was killed almost immediately. The soldiers fled northwest back toward the hills. The wagons were circled, and fallen horses became breastworks. Firing continued all day, and when it was over, fifty men were killed or wounded, including most of the officers.[19]

Joe Rankin made a twenty-eight hour dash to Rawlins to report the battle. On October 1, 1879, the garrison at Fort D. A. Russell heard that the Utes nearly wiped out a detachment on the Milk River. The War Department ordered Colonel Wesley Merritt to move from Fort Russell (near Cheyenne) via the Union Pacific Railroad to Fort Steele. Merritt was ordered to take 200 cavalry and 150 infantry to Milk River so as to relieve Captain Payne.[20] The confusion was compounded by Denver newspapers that reported an uprising on the Southern Ute (Los Pinos) Reservation.

Captain F. S. Dodge, stationed in Middle Park with his Ninth Cavalry, was ordered on October 1 to relieve Thornburgh. He arrived October 2 and reinforced the besieged troops. Meanwhile, Merritt, moving south, arrived October 5, only to discover that the fight was over.[21] The Utes withdrew in the face of this force.

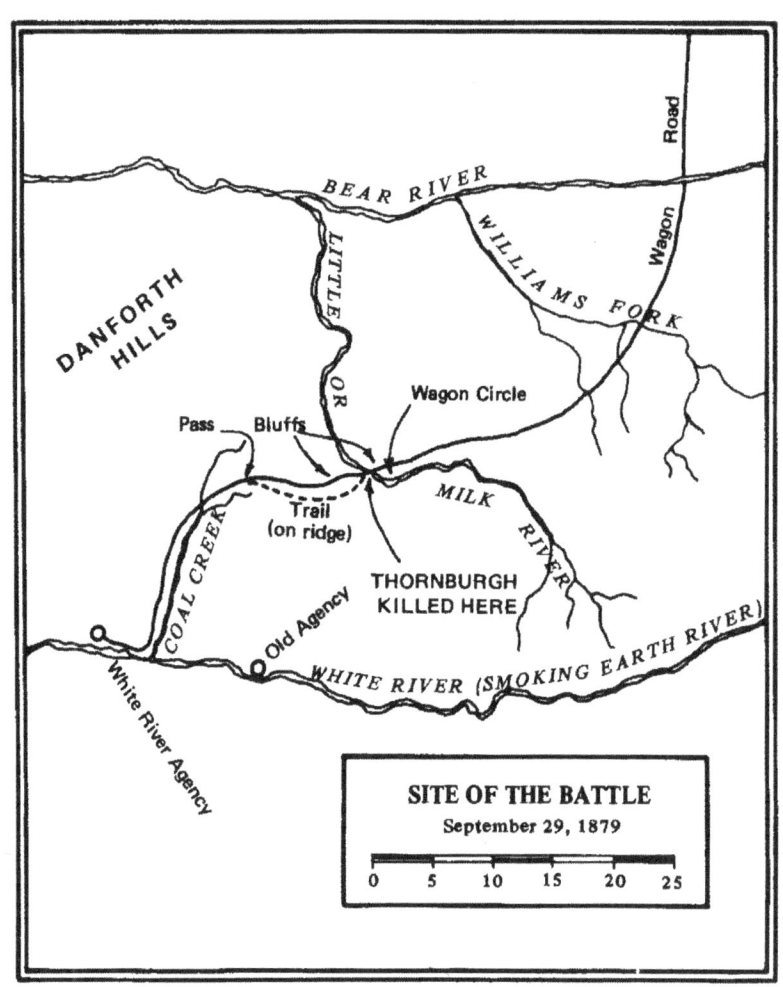

Site of Thornburgh Battle, September 29, 1879
From Robert Emmitt, *The Last War Trail*, page 201

Thornburgh Monument, 1981
Photo by F.J. Athearn

While the Thornburgh detachment was beseiged, White River Agency was also attacked by the Utes. On the night of September 30, 1879, agency Indians rose up and killed all eleven white males at White River. Meeker was killed and his body pierced by a barrel stave. The Utes then took hostage Mrs. Meeker, Josephine, Mrs. Shadrack Price and her two children.[22]

It was not until October 13, 1879, that the newspapers got their first dispatches describing the agency massacre portrayed by Merritt, second on the scene. The headlines blazed, "A SCENE OF SLAUGHTER," and Denver citizens demanded immediate action. Governor Pitkin denounced the attack in no uncertain terms, and incidentally pointed out that 12,000,000 acres could be opened with the removal of the Utes.[23] Herein lay the perfect opportunity to be rid of the natives for good.

The Ute uprising came to an end when Chief Ouray sent a message to the Northern Utes to lay down their arms. Douglas, Colorow, Johnson, and others fled into the hills where they awaited the outcome of negotiations with Ouray. Former Indian Agent, General Charles Adams, working with Ouray, managed to secure release of the captives. None of the hostages were harmed, and Josephine actually praised the humane treatment they received.[24]

The Utes were initially provoked, but despite the decent treatment of the hostages and regardless of Douglas' attempts at peace, Colorado's citizens demanded "the Utes Must Go." The outcome of the Meeker Massacre was a commission established to investigate the cause, and punish those who were guilty. The commission had only the captive women as eye-witnesses, and Ouray refused to let them testify (under Ute law their testimony was null and void). Ouray demanded a trial in Washington, D.C., where he felt the natives would get a fair hearing. Since the commission did not have such authority, Douglas and several minor chiefs were placed on a train for Fort Leavenworth, Kansas, on the pretext that they were going to Washington. The Ute chiefs were held in jail at Leavenworth for several years. This was the extent of the punishment for the Utes who took part in the uprising.[25]

More importantly, the rebellion provided the reason for final removal of the Utes. In 1880, a delegation of Utes headed by Ouray left for Washington. A treaty was put together by which the Utes lost all of their western Colorado lands. The natives were given two reservations. The Southern Utes got the La Plata Reservation, while the Northern Utes moved into Utah to the Uintah Reservation. In addition, they were given $60,000 in back annuities, and $50,000 in new annuities. Three-fourths of the males of the Ute Tribe had to sign the treaty before it became effective.[26]

On August 20, 1880, Ouray died, and the Utes lost one of their best spokesmen. However, despite his influence among Europeans, it is doubtful that he could have saved the Utes from removal. In that same year, General R. S. Mackenzie with six companies of cavalry and nine companies of infantry from Fort Garland, began moving the Ute nation out of northwestern Colorado. There were only about 1,500 people, and on September 7, 1881, the last of the Utes passed the Grand and Gunnison River junction and headed into Utah. The next year, 1882, Congress declared the vacated Ute lands open for filing, and what were hunting grounds became available for agriculture and ranching.[27]

The causes for the Meeker Massacre were many and complex, but the basic problem was a total lack of understanding between two cultures. A series of preventable events transpired to create an atmosphere for trouble. The worst offenders in the Ute removal were the people of Colorado, who found the perfect excuse to get rid of the Utes and to take their land. Because of the uprising of 1879, the balance of northwest Colorado was cleared of Indians, and the corner was open to all comers. As Senator Nathaniel Hill of Colorado so ably stated, the injustice done to the Ute was inexcusable, but the year 1879 signaled a new era in western Colorado.

NOTES ON CHAPTER 5

1. See: Robert Berkhofer, *Salvation and the Savage,* (Seattle: University of Washington Press, 1965).

2. See: Robert Emmitt, *The Last War Trail,* (Norman: University of Oklahoma Press, 1955) and Marshall Sprague, *Tragedy at White River* (Boston: Little, Brown, 1957) for general descriptions by modern writers of the events leading up to the Ute removal. Other sources include: Elizabeth Nixon, "Meeker Massacre. . . . ," (Greeley, Colo.: Colorado State Teacher's College, 1935), Master's Thesis; T. L. Iden, "History of the Ute Indian Cessions of Colorado," (Gunnison, Colo.: Western State College, 1928), Master's Thesis; Agnes E. Spiva, "Utes in Colorado," (Boulder, Colo. University of Colorado, 1929), Master's Thesis; J. P. Boyd, *Recent Indian Wars,* (n.l, n.p., 1891); Thomas F. Dawson, *The Ute War,* (Boulder, Colo.; Johnson Publishing 1964); and Al Look, *Last Stand at White River and Milk Creek, Western Colorado in 1879,* (Denver; Golden Bell Press, 1972). The *Colorado Magazine* contains a number of articles regarding the Utes. See Page 276 of the *Colorado Magazine Index,* 1921-1948.

3. Emmitt, op. cit., p. 26.

4. Sprague, op. cit., p. 167.

5. Emmitt, op. cit., p. 53. See also: Nathan C. Meeker, *Letter to the Secretary of the Interior, 1879* (Washington, D.C.: Government Printing Office, 1880).

6. Letter quoted in Emmitt, op. cit., pp. 53-54.

7. Ibid., p. 55 and Sprague, op. cit., p. 143.

8. Sprague, op. cit., p. 176.

9. Emmitt, op. cit., pp. 56-68.

10. Meeker, op. cit., p. 71.

11. Ibid., p. 2.

12. As detailed in Emmitt, op. cit., pp. 87-90.

13. Sprague, op. cit., p. 120.

14. Emmitt, op. cit., pp. 149-151.

15. As quoted in Emmitt, op. cit., p. 155.

16. Wesley Merritt, "Three Indian Campaigns," Harper's New Monthly, Magazine, April, 1890, pp. 720-737, and Ibid., p. 166.

17. *Meeker to Thronburgh,* September 27, 1879, as quoted in Emmitt, op. cit., p. 187.

18. As described in Merritt and the Indian Wars, (London: Johnson-Trauton: Military Press, 1972).

19. Merritt, op. cit., p. 732. Also described in: Maria B. Kimball, *A Soldier-Doctor of our Army*, (n. 1., n. p., 1917).

20. Ibid., p. 733.

21. Emmitt, op. cit., p. 221.

22. As quoted from Emmitt, Ibid., pp. 233-234.

23. Frederick Pitkin, quoted in the Denver *Daily News*, October 13, 1879.

24. See: Josephine Meeker, *The Ute Massacre!*, (Philadelphia: Old Franklin Publishing Co.: 1879).

25. Emmitt, op. cit., pp. 282-287.

26. Sprague, op. cit., p. 315. See also: *Committee on Indian Affairs U.S. Congress*, (Washington, D.C.: Government Printing Office, 1880), 46th Congress, Session 2, House Document, Misc. no. 38 and U.S. White River Ute Commission, (U.S. Congress, 56th 2nd Session, Executive Document 83, 1880).

27. Sprague, op. cit., p. 329.

Chapter 6

SETTLEMENT IN MIDDLE PARK

AND THE YAMPA VALLEY

Prior to Ute removal, western Colorado was of intense interest to potential settlers and speculators. Middle Park, one of the areas earliest settled west of the divide, saw new development in the 1870s, while far western Colorado was prepared for further settlement by a series of surveys that occurred beginning in 1871 and lasted until 1876. These inventories were the last major western mapping operations, and were conducted by the newly created United States Geological Survey (USGS), under the direction of Dr. Ferdinand V. Hayden.

Hayden began his team surveys with Middle Park in 1871. The work included a detailed description of the geology of the park, an appendix that provided details on flora and fauna, and a physical topographic survey (made by A. R. Marvine). He drew no conclusions as to the value of the Park.[1] A year later, the Grand River valley was explored by A. C. Peale who created a detailed geologic report on the area. At the same time, Gustavus R. Beckler surveyed the geology of South and Middle Parks. A topography of the Grand River valley was done by Henry Gannett in 1875.

In 1876 results of the northwestern Colorado surveys were published. Geology for the area was provided by C. A. White, while A. D. Wilson did topography. F. M. Endlich wrote a geology essay for the White River section, while George Chittenden provided topography for the White River. Gustavus Beckler wrote topographic descriptions of the Yampa Valley. This survey included Beckler's North Park descriptions and lands over to the Utah-Colorado line.[2]

The 1876 survey showed that North Park had some 700 square miles of grazing lands having agricultural potential.[3] The Hayden party noted that Douglas and Piceance Creeks were constant, but other subsidiary creeks could not be relied upon, which made agriculture in the Piceance Basin risky.[4] They concluded that the Yampa Valley and Egeria Park were good grazing regions, while the Little Snake River area was "well watered grassland."[5] The party noted that agriculture was possible in that "Mr. Danforth has cultivated about forty acres of land for the use of the agency..." This referred to Reverend Danforth's efforts at the White River Agency where he was growing potatoes, turnips, beets, and carrots in 1876.[6]

The Hayden survey of this region consisted of a sample of 800 square miles, that took ten days to survey. This would seem like a rather small sample of land. However, the group managed to look at most of the major geologic features of the area, and they triangulated most of the northwest corner with remarkable accuracy. The conclusions drawn from the surveys were that agriculture would be difficult without irrigation, and that the land was useful only near river valleys where grazing could take place. The Hayden survey provided the first solid information on this area since Fremont's and Powell's expeditions. Through publication of such information, prospective settlers were apprised of the value of the land.

Hayden did little to help settlement for in 1876 he wrote that the region was: "...nearly all uninhabitable both winter and summer..." Hayden notwithstanding, settlers moved into this "worthless" region.[7]

During the Hayden surveys a major scandal occurred in far western Colorado. In 1872 a reported discovery of "diamonds" in the region precipitated a major mining investment boom, and this swindle was of such quality and magnitude that many prominent men became involved in it. The plot revolved around Phillip Arnold and John Slack, who came to San Francisco with a sackful of raw "diamonds." The stones were carefully shown to the "right people", and it was intimated that a huge field existed somewhere in the Rockies.[8]

Slack and Arnold disappeared and then reappeared; they soon were bought out for $600,000 and the New York and San Francisco Mining and Commercial Company was founded by such luminaries as Grenville Dodge, General George McClellan, and Ben Butler to exploit these supposed resources. But there were skeptics. To quiet fears, the company hired Henry Janin, whose reputation was unquestioned when it came to evaluating mining potential; Janin looked at the goods and pronounced them real.[9] This was the beginning of a rush to northwest Colorado. It was hinted that diamonds were in the San Luis Valley, but the Laramie *Sentinel* scooped Colorado papers, when it determined that the field was in southern Wyoming or northern Colorado.[10] In addition, Clarence King, head of the United States Geological Survey, was drawn into the "find," and he had approved it.

In the fall of 1872 a serious search for the gem field began. Samuel F. Emmons of the USGS started to work with what little information he had, and soon concluded that what is now called Diamond Peak was the probable site. Emmons and his party worked in the Green and Yampa valleys seeking the field; they found little but coal.[11] However, Emmons did finally find gems, mostly rubies, on the north side of the peak. Within hours, mining claims were scattered all over the mountain. However, upon further investigation, the Emmons group found that the stones were planted near anthills, that showed signs of disturbance. Soon they gathered enough evidence to indicate that fraud had been perpetrated. It was not until November 1872, that King released the news that the "diamond fields" were a hoax. The company that was created collapsed, and $350,000 in invested funds disappeared. King and the USGS got some glory from this fraud - many miners and mining communities noted that thanks to the Geological Survey, events like this could be prevented. In exposing the fraud, King helped set the stage for new USGS work in the West; people felt that the government was doing something to protect the public interest.

Middle Park and Egeria Park were developing rapidly into cattle and ranch lands by the mid-1870s. As noted, William Byers tried to develop Hot Sulphur Springs into a resort during the early 1860s; however, due to a lack of good roads, not much happened. Middle

Park was finally opened in 1873, when John Q. A. Rollins constructed a wagon road over Rollins Pass. This toll road led from South Boulder Creek over the Continental Divide and down to the Winter Park area. It was a well-built road, and usable most of the year. Rollins charged $2.50 per wagon, and because of this construction, Middle Park saw a new flow of settlers. That same year provided the creation of Grand County, with Byers, Rollins, and Porter M. Smart in the lead. With the establishment of a county, Middle Park became civilized to a point that some towns actually sprang up. Byers drew up his plans for the town of Hot Sulphur Springs in 1873, while other small ranches were destined to become towns.[12]

Middle Park, now Grand County, saw a number of land filings take place. Hilery Harris filed for a ranch in 1874, while Tracy C. Tyler claimed land at the site of Kremmling as early as 1865. John Himebaugh took out a claim, as did the McQueary family. The Humphrey and Green families soon arrived. In 1875 Henry King took out land along Troublesome Creek. In July 1875, Barney Day arrived to claim a ranch along the same creek. He was the father of the first European child born in the Park in July, 1876.[13]

However, despite the number of families coming into the Park, the main trade was still summer tourism. It was estimated that in August 1874, between 200 and 300 visitors were in the area. They scattered out from Grand Lake to Hot Sulphur Springs. In fact, trade was so good that Byers built a second hotel at the Springs that same year. While Byers expanded his holdings, Rollins bought land near the Fraser River to raise hay. Here he built the Junction House near the site of present-day Tabernash.[14] Porter Smart also tried to cash in on the boom by organizing the Bear River Colonization and Improvement Company to import settlers, an operation that came to naught.

In that same year the Berthoud Pass road was rebuilt and opened to traffic. The major figure behind this revitalization was Lewis Gaskill, who finally settled in Middle Park. The Berthoud Road was soon recognized as superior to Rollins Pass, and by 1880 Rollins' Road was in ruins. Berthoud Pass provided better transportation into the Park. In 1875 mail service began over the Pass, and in 1876 a regular stage run was inaugurated by the Colorado Stage Company by Bela Hughes and Ben Holladay, owners.[15]

Lewis Gaskill was destined to become one of the major figures in the Park, for he discovered gold in the region. In 1879 a minor boom occured when gold ores were found near Teller City. From it arose a series of towns including Teller City, Lulu City, and Burnett. These little camps showed great promise during the early '80s, but by 1885 the rush was over, and the towns died for lack of mineral resources. The census of 1885 shows the population of Grand County at only fifteen.[16]

Mining was not solely to blame for the depletion of population. A threat of Ute Indians remained until after 1879. In fact, over 100,000 acres of timber were burned in 1878, and a number of settlers fled. Yet a few remained; William Cozens established the first post office in Fraser in 1876 and stayed through the various problems, while the King family was still there in 1885. Yet, Middle Park, an area that had shown so much promise, was virtually dead by 1885.

View of Meeker, Colorado, about 1905
Photo by H.S. Gale, USGS

With Middle Park slowly filling up, other settlers continued to press westward. In 1876 James H. Crawford's family settled in the Steamboat Springs area. This became the site of modern-day Steamboat Springs. Other than a few miners at Hahn's Peak, the upper end of the Yampa Valley remained unsettled. Egeria Park was occupied to a limited extent as early as 1882, but these people were primarily in the ranching business, and many of them moved northward to Steamboat. Egeria Park's first permanent settler was Bernard Spunk, who came to the area in 1882. The next year a post office was opened at his ranch.[18]

Farther west a few ranches appeared. With this industry came small settlements that usually contained a post office and a supply store. Such trading posts catered to local ranchers (of whom there were few), and until late 1879, to the Utes in the region. That there was settlement is evidenced in George Crofutt's listing of towns (usually post offices) as of 1881.[19] In northwestern Colorado the following "towns" were found:

Town	County
Axial	Routt
Egeria (Park)	Routt
Edith	Routt
Fraser	Grand
Hahn's Peak	Routt
Hayden	Routt
Hot Sulphur Springs	Grand
Lay	Routt
Lulu (City)	Grand
Maybell	Routt
Meeker	Routt
Middle (Park)	Routt
North Park	Grand
Rangely	Routt
Slater	Routt
Steamboat Springs	Routt
Teller (City)	Grand
Troublesome	Grand
Walden	Grand
Yampa	Routt

The western slope of Colorado was indeed being occupied but the so-called "towns" were widely scattered. Weekly mail service to Rawlins, Wyoming, was important as was a semiregular stage run. Crofutt notes that all lines led from Rawlins. For example, he notes that Axial was 135 miles from Rawlins and the stage fare was twenty-two dollars, one way.[20] He stated that Hayden was 122 miles from Rawlins, while Rangely was so isolated that it had no mail service. Most of the towns were stock raising supply centers, and Crofutt concluded that they had little real potential for growth.[21]

Towns Often Grew out of Ranches
USGS Photo

North Park also saw settlement during the mid-1870s. J. O. Pinkham (after whom Pinkhampton was named) brought cattle into the Park in 1874 or 1875. He used the natural abundance of wild hay to feed his stock, while at the same time he sold some to settlers in Middle Park.[22] Across the Park Range, Steamboat Springs' main crop was also wild hay, which was shipped to Wyoming for transport back East on the Union Pacific.[23]

By the mid-1880s, Middle, North, and Egeria Parks were settled. Cattle and hay were the main industries, although some coal was being mined in the Oak Creek and Steamboat Springs region for local consumption.

Steamboat Springs became the unofficial "capital" of the northwest by the late 1880s. The townsite itself was laid out in 1884 by James Crawford. The Steamboat Springs Townsite Company was capitalized at $160,000, and soon after formal organization, merchants began to appear. The Steamboat *Pilot* newspaper was founded in 1885, while the first general store was incorporated in 1886 by Milner and Company. A few years earlier a mail route from Steamboat to Hayden had been established, when a small mining rush occurred along Fortification Creek. Placer gold was found in 1882, but the boom died out, and little else developed in that area. Steamboat, having a newspaper, a series of stores, and by 1889 a stage line to Russell's Siding (Wolcott), became the largest town in the area. It was estimated that 500 people resided in Steamboat Springs.[24]

Further development of this area awaited better transportation. New mineral deposits also helped to restimulate the Yampa Valley. To the west the cattle industry was dominant, and most cattlemen were careful to keep the range to themselves. Such names as Iles, Hoy, Rash, and Haley dominated northwestern Colorado's society, politics, and economic development.

NOTES FOR CHAPTER 6

1. Ferdinand V. Hayden, *United States Geologic Survey of the Territories, Annual Report*, 1st-12th, (Washington: Government Printing Office, 1867-1878, 12 Vols., 1873) p. 81.

2. Ibid., Vol. for 1875.

3. Ibid., Vol. for 1876, p. 344.

4. Ibid., Vol. for 1876, p. 346.

5. Ibid., Vol. for 1876, p. 347.

6. Ibid., Vol. for 1876, p. 353.

7. Ferdinand V. Hayden, "Explorations Made in Colorado," *American Naturalist*, Vol. XI, Number 2, 1877, pp. 73-86.

8. Richard A. Bartlett, *Great Surveys of the American West*, (Norman: University of Oklahoma Press, 1962), p. 187.

9. Ibid., p. 189.

10. Ibid., p. 202.

11. Ibid., p. 203.

12. Robert C. Black, *Island in the Rockies*, (Boulder, Colo: Pruett Press, 1969), p. 85. See also: Louise C. Harrison, *Empire and the Berthoud Pass*, (Denver: Big Mountain Press, 1964); Mary L. Cairns, *Grand Lake: The Pioneers*, (Denver, World Press, 1946). Mary L. Cairns, *The Olden Days: A Companion Book to Grand Lake: The Pioneers*, (Denver: World Press, 1954), and Cora Belle Oberholtzer, "The Grazing Industry of Middle Park, Colorado," Boulder, Colo.: University of Colorado, 1942), M.A. Thesis.

13. Black, op. cit., p. 101 and Harrison, op. cit., p. 91.

14. Black, op. cit., p. 109.

15. Harrison, op. cit., p. 270.

16. Cairns, op. cit., pp. 99-105 and Black, op. cit., pp. 152-159.

17. Cairns, op. cit., p. 104, and Black op. cit., p. 158.

18. Charles Leckenby, *The Tread of Pioneers*, (Steamboat Springs, Colo.: Steamboat *Pilot*, 1944), pp. 120-121, See also: Clark C. Ewing, Pamela Berude, and Margaret C. Ewing, *Early McCoy, A Hundred Years Perspective*, (Glenwood Springs, Colo.: Raymond's Printers, 1976), John Ambos, *McCoy Memoirs*, (n.l, n.p., 1976). and Perry Ault, *From Oxen to Jet Planes*, (Steamboat Springs, Colo.: Steamboat *Pilot*, 1971).

Chapter 7

DEVELOPMENT OF THE

CATTLE AND SHEEP INDUSTRY

While the west slope was developing during the 1870s, the far western side of the state was also undergoing major changes. Construction of the Union Pacific Railroad through Wyoming introduced new economic realities to the area. The crews needed beef, and while buffalo supplied by hunters was substantial, it was not nearly enough; beef was demanded and suppliers were quick to fill the desires of the workmen.

The father of the cattle industry in Wyoming was Judge William Carter of Fort Bridger, who began to ship Texas Longhorns by rail to Fort Bridger in 1868; that place had recently been reached by the Union Pacific. He also imported a carload of Shorthorns to improve the breed.[1]

By 1871 the first cattle were driven into northwest Colorado. The winter of 1871-72 was one of the worst on record; few spots of open range were to be found on the western range. A New Mexican cattleman named George Baggs trailed 900 steers from southern Colorado into Brown's Hole during November and by spring he had not lost a single head. Baggs' partner, William Crawford, after talking it over with Baggs, decided to locate in the Brown's Hole region, and raise cattle on the lush native grasses of the valley. Brown's Hole was considered ideal for cattle raising, but it had its disadvantages too. The "Hole" was long used by fur trappers, and then later by bandits, who could hide in the valley with no fear of being caught. It was the watering place for several well-known outlaws, such as "Mexican Joe" Herrera and the Tip Gault Gang.[2]

Danger notwithstanding, rancher settlers found their way into Brown's Park. In 1874 W. G. Tittsworth and Griff Edwards drove several hundred head of cattle into the valley, but they were soon forced out by the partnership of Jesse and Valentine Hoy. The Hoys were dominant cattlemen in the Park by 1876, exceeded only by the Baggs' group. Along with the big ranchers, there were other settlers like Jimmie Reed, and Sam Bassett.

The Brown's Park region became notorious because of constant rustling going on within the valley. The center of this illegal activity seemed to be the Bassett ranch. In addition to common cattle theft, other problems cropped up in the valley. It was a hide-out for several nationally famous gangs, including Butch Cassidy (George LeRoy Parker) and his gang, the Matt Warner Gang, Elza Lay, Cassidy's right-hand man, and various other desperados.[3]

The Cassidy gang worked out of the Park and Utah until the early 1900s when the Union Pacific Railroad, along with the famous "Rolling Posse" drove them out of the country.[4]

Brown's Park was not the only area that opened to cattle. The Little Snake and Yampa Valleys became major stock centers. George Baggs moved his outfit up the Little Snake into Wyoming, where he found the land between Fortification and Savery Creeks more to his liking. Here he put up a ranch building that eventually became the nucleus of Baggs, Wyoming. Baggs was the merchandising center of northwestern Colorado until the advent of Craig; it was nearly dead center between the Yampa Valley and the Union Pacific line at Rawlins. For many years Baggs was the primary cattle town of the region until it was finally superseded by Steamboat Springs when the Denver and Salt Lake Railroad reached that city in 1909. Baggs not only left his name on the map, so did his common-law wife, Maggie, after whom Maggie's Nipple, a butte in the northwestern corner, is named.[5]

Other little settlements, mainly ranches, sprang up in the area. Such places as Lay, Maybell, and Hayden became cattle centers, devoted to providing mail service and merchandise to cattlemen. The major ranchers in the Yampa Valley were Ora Haley, the Carey Brothers, Jim Norvell, Pat Cullen, Si Dawson, and others. They saw to it that their spreads took most of the available rangelands. The 1880s, 1890s, and early 1900s were the heydays of open range cattle. This meant that cows were put out on the range year-round, and in winter they depended on native forage for survival; in some years this could be a profitable venture, while in others, many stockmen went broke. The Little Snake, Yampa, and White River valleys were generally good for range cattle, while the lands north and south of these river valleys were marginal. Where water was available regularly, there was usually no problem; but in the dry northern section, cattle fared poorly. North Park cattle were in much the same position as far northwestern cattle.

The Cattle Industry was the Mainstay of the Region
for Many Years, *Colorado State Historical Society*

This area was also open range country, and here too, the hard winters often took terrible tolls on herds. However, the industry survived, thanks to credit and high prices. Many a cattleman was wiped out, but would go back again next year while the bank collected anywhere from 12 to 18 percent interest.[6]

The White River country was also a serious cattle producing area. From Meeker, stock was driven south through Douglas Canyon and over Douglas Pass to Rifle, Colorado, where they were shipped on the Denver and Rio Grande Railroad to Denver and points east. There was no road to Rifle until 1879. The JQS cattle trail (1885) was used to drive animals onto the Roan Cliffs and into the Piceance Basin.[7]

The great fear of western Colorado cattlemen was an invasion of sheep. The sheep industry was not new in Colorado. By the 1860s there were hundreds of thousands of head in the San Luis Valley and throughout southern Colorado. Cattlemen in the north considered themselves lucky that sheep had not moved onto their range. However, the inevitable was coming; the Meeker *Herald*, on January 14, 1888, warned that woolies were to be brought from Utah to White River's grazing areas, including the Axial Basin and the Iles Basin ares.[8] Frightened cattlemen prepared to meet the sheepmen at the border and turn them back, but the scare never materialized, and cattle remained supreme into the 1890's.

A first attempt to bring sheep into northwest Colorado's cattle country came in 1894, when Jack Edwards of Wyoming tried to move several thousand head in Routt County. Edwards claimed that he was being forced into Colorado because Tom Kinney's 75,000 head of sheep had driven his flocks out of Wyoming. A few local farmers favored importation of sheep to get rid of a surplus of hay that had accumulated in the valley, but the area's cattle barons refused to consider the admittance of sheep. A posse rode to the Wyoming border (near Dixon) and turned back Edwards' band.[9]

The primary complaint cattlemen had about sheep was that they allegedly grazed to the roots and prevented cattle from getting enough grass, in addition to not permitting the range to grow back. Cattlemen also argued that sheep and cattle could not mix together, because the smell of sheep was so bad that cattle panicked when the woolies were near. About the only truth in the various stories was that sheep may graze to the roots.

Sheep wars broke out in Routt County, and later in Rio Blanco County, during the late 1890s. However, prior to this time, cattle raisers had problems with rustlers. Numerous cattlemen's associations were formed to deal with the problem. The most notorious example of hired guns came with the formation of the Yampa Valley Cattle Growers Association. This bunch engaged Tom Horn, a cowardly paid assassin, to exterminate suspected rustlers, a job that he did with relish. Horn killed Isom Dart, a well-known cattleman. Matt Rash, one of the founders of a cattlemen's association in

Brown's Park, was ambushed by Horn.[10] In addition to cleaning up suspected cattle rustlers in the region, cattlemen's associations tried to eliminate predators, and in some cases, competition. One of the best examples of smaller ranchers ganging up on big outfits was the establishment of the Snake River Association, using the OVO brand. This group was dedicated to marketing on a cooperative basis, and competing with ranches like Ora Haleys much-hated Two Bar outfit.[11]

In 1902 the Brown's Park Ranchmen's Association was formed to combat grey wolves. They offered a bounty of $20 per hide. In North Park an association was created for the same purpose in 1903.[12]

If cattlemen did not have enough problems with rustlers, sheepmen, and predators, another crisis occurred in 1891 when the White River Timber Reserve was created. This withdrew some 750,000 acres of prime Federal grazing land. Now cattlemen had to get grazing permits, and even worse, they competed with sheepmen for the right to use the pastures.[13] The White River Reserve was expanded in 1907 to 1,133,330 acres, which made grazing lands harder to obtain. The other factor that influenced the cattle industry was the Forest Homestead Act of 1906 by which forest grazing lands could be filed on. Actually, due to the extreme care of the Agriculture Department, only 177,000 acres were ever claimed.[14]

Most of the intraindustry cattle conflicts were between smaller cattle outfits and the large companies. By 1912 the U.S. Forest Service and the small cattle companies were able to out-maneuver larger cattlemen, such as Ora Haley. This marked the end of open range operations. Carefully controlled grazing was now the rule.[15] In desperation, cattlemen (of the large companies) began to harass settlers who were homesteading grazing lands, (such as a colony of Swedes who were dryland farming several mesas in Routt County), and sheep owners who gained grazing permits from the Forest Service.

The Routt County range wars reached new depths in 1911 with the George Woolley Sheep Massacre, when several hundred sheep were "rimrocked" by driving them over a cliff. The citizens of Routt County were outraged by the crime, and although the perpetrators were never caught, sheep growers gained much sympathy. The war degenerated to the use of strychnine on sheep in 1913. Yet by 1915 sheep were grazing in Routt National Forest (having been brought into Whiskey Park in 1910), and in 1920 the Northwest Sheepgrowers Association was formed for mutual protection.

The year 1920 marked culmination of the sheep wars, when the Battle of Yellowjacket Pass, located between Craig and Meeker, occurred between sheepmen and cattle interests. The Colorado state militia was called in to restore order.[16]

In 1934 the Taylor Grazing Service was created to control grazing (and overgrazing) on public lands other than forest withdrawals. This service allotted lands to cattlemen, sheep raisers, and others for grazing purposes. For all practical purposes, the balance of public domain was withdrawn in northwestern Colorado by this Act, and the era of the open range ended. Equally the era of homesteading was closed forever. In 1946 the General Land Office, original caretaker of public lands, and the Taylor Grazing Service, were merged as the Bureau of Land Management. This organization continues to issue grazing permits among many other duties and generally keeps the public domain from being overused.

Northwestern Colorado's cattle industry boomed when transportation came to the Yampa Valley. Prior to the building of the Denver, Northwestern, and Pacific Railroad, cattle were shipped either to Rawlins, Wyoming, for transshipment on the Union Pacific, or they were driven to Wolcott, Colorado, along the Denver and Rio Grande Railroad, where they were transferred to Denver and points east. The Wyoming route was preferred, as it was not as hard on cattle as trying to drive them down the Yampa Valley, over the Gore Range, and onto the railhead. Losses were more severe using the Wolcott or Rifle routes than when driven north. However, by 1909 Steamboat Springs had rail service, and it became the largest shipper in Colorado's northwestern corner. In fact, at one point, it was the greatest cattle shipping point in the United States.[17]

Another major factor changing the cattle industry of this region was an introduction, in the early 1900s, of new breeding stock. Cattlemen found that markets demanded more than stringy Longhorns. Most Texas cattle were Longhorns that had various defects, such as peculiar diseases that affected their ability to gain weight. Cattlemen in the northwest corner proceeded to import special breeds such as Shorthorns and Herefords to improve the weight-gaining ability of Longhorns.[18]

Using hay to winterfeed cattle came during the late 1890s and early 1900s in this region. Range cattle did not always survive winters due to lack of ground forage. There was an abundance of top quality wild hay in the Yampa Valley and also in North Park. By 1900 both of these areas used this natural resource to winterfeed cattle. Further, North Park cattlemen learned that cattle close-herded, and fed on hay, would bring better market prices.

Thanks to the need for hay, a new industry was developed; wild hay soon turned into a domestic product. North Park became famous for its quality hay, and thousands of tons were exported yearly from the Park to Denver and other eastern cities. Even horsemen from Kentucky specified North Park hay. Balers came into use during the 1890s when a North Park cowboy named Joe Lawrence invented a way to use horses to pull a hayrack that would bale automatically; this revolutionized the industry and production soared. The Yampa Valley produced equally good native hay.[19]

One of the basic cultural conflicts that arose between the cattle industry, sheep men, and farming interests was that of land ownership. Nearly all the grazing area involved was public land administered by the General Land Office (GLO). This public domain was open to any who could pay a filing fee, and who would stay on it for five years. When the first cattlemen cam in, they simply assumed that grazing was the only realistic land use and that no one would try to settle the area. For about twenty years this remained true, and cattlemen came to feel the land they used was theirs, not public. As time wore on and increased demands for lands were heard, even marginal land was settled. Additionally, cattlemen were pressured by sheep raisers to share the land. Homesteaders claimed land that cattle interests felt was theirs by right of prior claim. The conflicts that arose were often violent, and cattle owners were loath to give up what they saw as theirs by right of first occupation. This type of philosophy is still strong in many parts of the modern west.

Pressures increased and the attitude of most Americans at the time was that land must be used; it must provide profit. After all, why not use land that was seized from the "indolent Indians" to its fullest extent? Cattlemen had already abused nature by overgrazing and over-stocking. Now, just when the land was marginal for cattle, homesteaders and sheepmen wanted to recast its use. Sheep would graze what was left and leave a barren plain, while homesteaders would turn over the virgin sod, plant it, and hope that a crop would grow. No matter how one viewed it, the land was not fit for this use. Perhaps cattlemen realized this more than most, but increased demands caused them to engage in open conflict with those who would occupy their ranges. This cultural conflict lasted from the 1890s to 1920, when the open range cattle industry died of its own accord.[20]

The cattle industry of northwestern Colorado was the mainstay of the economy until 1920. Since cattle were the prime commodity in the area, it was natural that cattlemen were key figures in politics, the economy, and in society. The land was cattle land, and people were there because of cattle. In 1904 it was estimated that the value of cattle in Routt County was $836,410, or more than half the total assessed valuation of the county.[21]

Cattle remained the largest single industry in the region until the 1920s when other industries such as coal, oil, and sheep threatened to overtake that industry.

NOTES FOR CHAPTER 7

1. John Rolfe Burroughs, *Where the Old West Stayed Young,* (New York: Morrow, 1962), p. 10. See also: Ernest S. Osgood, *The Day of the Cattlemen,* (Chicago: University of Chicago Press, 1929) and Maurice Frink, *When Grass was King,* (Boulder, Colo.: University of Colorado, 1956).

2. Burroughs, op. cit., p. 16 and p. 23.

3. Ibid., pp. 114-126.

4. Ibid., p. 127 and "Butch Cassidy's Early Exploits Recalled," The Denver *Post,* September 27, 1972.

5. Burroughs, op. cit., p. 11 and p. 81.

6. As related in both Burroughs and Osgood.

7. CWA Interviews, *Rio Blanco County, 1933.* Documents 31-32, in Colorado Historical Society, Denver, Colorado.

8. Meeker *Herald,* January 14, 1888, p. 1, Meeker, Colorado.

9. Edward N. Wentworth, "Sheep Wars of the 90s in Northwest Colorado," in *Denver Westerners Brandbook,* (Denver: Denver Westerners, 1946), p. 135.

10. Daniel Tyler, "F.R. Carpenter, Routt County, 1900-1920," (Fort Collins, Colorado State University, 1967), M.A. Thesis, p. 14 and in Burroughs, op. cit., pp. 204-216 and pp. 216-225.

11. Tyler, op. cit., p. 21.

12. Payne, op. cit., p. 310.

13. Ibid., p. 34.

14. Ibid., p. 42.

15. Ibid., p. 65.

16. Ibid., pp. 71-72 and pp. 124-125.

17. John Rolfe Burroughs, *Steamboat in the Rockies,* (Fort Collins: Old Army Press, 1974), p. 160.

18. Payne, op. cit., p. 178.

19. Worster, op. c.

20. Payne, op. cit., p. 123.

21. Tyler, op. cit., p. 15.

Chapter 8

MINING AND TRANSPORTATION

1890 - 1920

The western slope of Colorado experienced several mineral booms in the late nineteenth and early twentieth centuries. These rushes were different than earlier ones in that most of the minerals involved were not precious.

One of the bigger discoveries occurred in far west Colorado and in eastern Utah. The mineral, gilsonite, was discovered during the late 1870s by Samuel Gilson of Salt Lake City. Gilsonite is an oil and tar-based rock that can be processed into asphalt. At first the market was limited to industrial uses, such as lining beer barrels to make them waterproof. In 1889 Gilson, who had been mining the mineral since 1886 at Dragon, Utah, sold his holdings to the Anheuser-Busch Brewing Company of St. Louis, who used gilsonite for beer barrels, and felt that it was better to own the source rather than to depend on a small operation such as Gilson's. In 1889 the Gilson Asphaltum Company was organized, and the Black Dragon Mine, near Dragon, was extensively developed. The major problem with gilsonite was that it was hard to ship; it was bulky and highly flammable. At first, mules carried the material to Salt Lake City, but this proved too expensive and soon wagons were engaged to haul loads over Baxter Pass to meet the Denver and Rio Grande Western Railroad at Mack, Colorado.[1]

View of Dragon, Utah, about 1906
Photo by H.S. Gale, USGS

With a change of management, new money was pumped into the industry. In 1903 the Barber Asphalt Company, owned by General Asphalt of New Jersey, capitalized the construction of a rail line from Dragon, Utah, to Mack, Colorado. The Uintah Railroad was projected as narrow gauge, and it would be built at a cost of $1.75 million; solely to haul gilsonite. The line which ran south from Dragon, over Baxter Pass and on to the Grand Valley, was finished in 1906.[2] In that same year, a toll road company was incorporated at Dragon to build roads to Vernal, Utah, and Rangely, Colorado, in order to provide stage and freight service.[3] It was hoped that the Uintah Railroad would be extended to both of these places. In 1913 a survey was made for a line to Meeker, Colorado, but nothing came of the effort.[4]

The rail line, sixty-two miles long, used specially-built Shay locomotives to pull flatcars of gilsonite over the long and steep Baxter Pass route. Along the right-of-way little towns and settlements sprang up, including places like Urado, East Vac, Columbine, Carbonera, Clarkton and Mack.[5] The line eventually ran from Watson, Utah, to Mack, Colorado. Hundreds of thousands of tons of gilsonite were hauled out and then processed. Asphalt was used not only for industrial purposes, but much of it went into streets across the nation when the age of highway building came in the 1920s.[6]

The Uintah Railway was unique in that it was built for one product, and gilsonite alone supported it. The railway also ran passenger service from Watson to Mack on a regular schedule. This was the first and only rail transportation on a north-south axis in far western colorado.

The Whiskey Creek Trestle is one of the few Remains
of the Uintah Railway, *H.A.E.R. Photo by F.J. Athearn*

Transporting gilsonite was tricky; it was so flammable that wet canvas sacks were used to keep the engine's sparks from setting it afire. In addition, wrecks from runaways, bad track, and landslides were common. During the 1930s, the advent of better roads and heavy trucks made the railroad obsolete, and it was finally abandoned in 1938. The old roadbed was converted into a county road and is still in use.[7] In 1957 a slurry pipeline was built from Watson to Mack and the gilsonite industry was a major factor in far western Colorado's economy until the plant at Fruita was converted to a gasoline refinery in the 1970s.[8]

Mining in North Park was also revitalized during the late 1890s. Gold mining took place on Independence Mountain from the 1870s but it was never a paying proposition. However, a few miners continually worked the area and tried to make a living. While prospecting this region, copper was found in the far northwest corner of the Park. A "boom" ensued and the town of Pearl, Colorado, was built. This copper discovery was not long lasting for it was over by 1915, but the mines stimulated growth in North Park. Copper was also discovered in Centennial Valley (Wyoming) and a minor rush occurred there too.[9]

View of Baxter Pass, 1981
Photo by F.J. Athearn

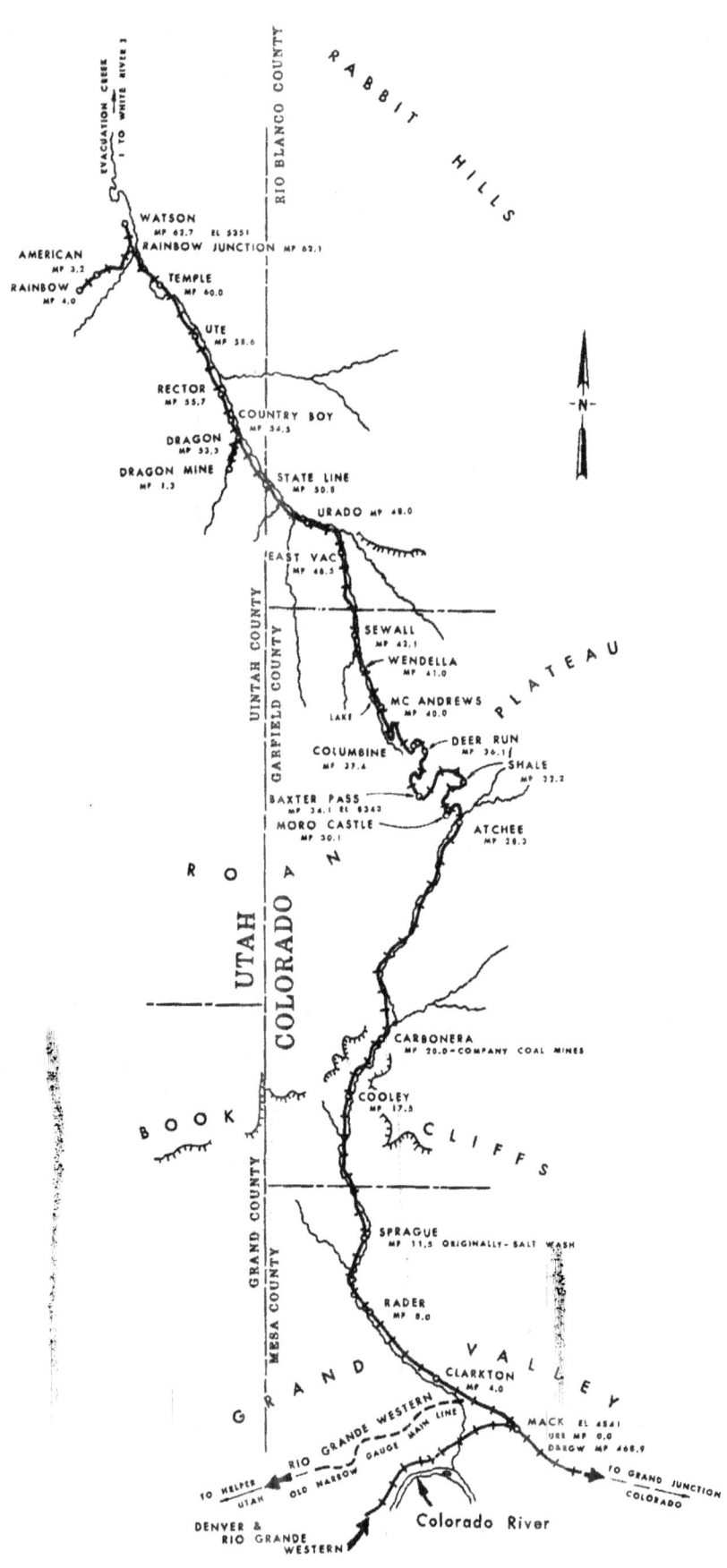

The Uintah Railway System as of 1935
The Uintah Railway: The Gilsonite Route, Bender

The other major mineral discovery that occurred in North Park was when the Riach Brothers discovered coal near Coalmont, Colorado, in 1890. Large quantities of this fuel were found in North Park, but development had to wait until transportation could be built. The coal was used locally until about 1911, when the Laramie, Hahn's Peak, and Pacific (LHPP) Railroad was constructed from Laramie, Wyoming, to Walden, Colorado. The Laramie, Hahn's Peak was projected to go over the Park Range, down the Elk River Valley, into Steamboat Springs, over to Craig, then on to Meeker, along the White River into Utah, and on to Salt Lake City. The road was built south to the Centennial Valley, reaching that area in 1906.[10] It had extended to Walden by 1911, and finally, the line reached Coalmont that same year. Coal reserves were thus tapped and the railroad brought cheap transportation to North Park.

The LHPP hoped that the Centennial and Pearl copper region, as well as the Coalmont coal fields, would provide revenues for operation. As it turned out, none of these sources except the coal fields proved to be of lasting worth. If there was a single major source traffic, it was cattle and freight. The Laramie, Hahn's Peak and Pacific suffered from chronic financial troubles, and went through several name changes. In 1907 it became the Laramie and Routt County Railway; in 1914 it was called the Colorado, Wyoming, and Eastern Railroad; and in 1924 the name was changed to the Northern Colorado and Eastern Railroad. That same year it was reincorporated into the Laramie, North Park and Western, which it remained until 1951 when the Union Pacific mercifully bought it out. The line remains today as the Union Pacific and still serves North Park to Walden. The Coalmont line has been removed.[11]

McAndrew's Lake was a Popular Tourist Spot on a
Hot Sunday Afternoon, *Photo by F.J. Athearn*

North Park was provided with rail service rather late; the only real benefit enjoyed by North Parkers was that freight service was cheaper and improved. The population of the area grew to a point that in 1912 the Park was made a separate county. Jackson County was carved out of Grand County and Walden was designated as the seat. A courthouse was built in 1912, and Walden became the leading town in the Park. Smaller towns like Cowdrey and Pinkhampton, were originally ranches that became post offices, while towns like Coalmont and Pearl were mining communities that acted as service centers. North Park's development after 1915 was primarily agricultural, with cattle and hay as the most important products. Coal production was marginal, but the discovery and tapping of this resource was of interest in that it marked potential development for other areas of western Colorado.

The far northwest corner of Colorado's mineral potential remained undeveloped except for a few minor discoveries. At Blue Mountain copper and some gold deposits were found, but they were much too small to provide the stimulus for a rush. Equally, gold placers along the Little Snake River and Timberlake Gulch were nearly worthless. Only Hahn's Peak continued as a viable mining area, and by 1900 even it was fading rapidly. However, the turn of the century saw the development of great interest in other mineral reserves. Hayden, in 1876, had noted the existence of coal, oil, and oil shale but due to the lack of demand and/or transportation, such fields were not tapped. By 1900 demands for coal had risen to the point that the western slope was being re-evaluated. Local Meeker residents long used coal from Streeter Canyon and some mining of oil shale took place around Meeker where the residents used it for fuel. Coal was also mined in this region; however, large scale mining did not occur until later.[12]

In 1906 the United States Geological Survey took a serious look at the Yampa Valley coal fields for the first time. It was known that coal existed, but the extent and the quality were still in question. A survey of the valley showed that major seams of coal were found at Oak Creek, Trout Creek, Twenty Mile Park, Wolf Creek, Sage Creek, Dry Creek, the Williams Fork area, Wollihan, Pilot Knob, and in the Flat Top Mountains.[13] It was noted that only one tenth of the area was in agricultural use, and therefore mining would not interfere with other industries. But the big problem was that there was no way to remove the coal cheaply. The surveyor, William Weston, noted that: "Without a railroad, no shipments of hay, grain, vegetables, or fruit can be made any more than can the coal."[14]

Later reports of the USGS in the area confirmed that the same problem existed; there were minerals in abundance but removing them would be difficult without transportation.

A 1906 USGS survey of the Yampa Valley by Nevin Fenneman concluded that high grade bituminous coal was readily available, but that a railroad would be needed to remove it.[15] The same old story; no transportation.

Northwestern Colorado in 1900 suffered from a severe lack of cheap and easy transport. Freight wagons and stagecoaches provided the only means of moving about the

84

region, and more isolated spots such as Rangely often had only semiregular service. As noted, most of the roads ran to the Rio Grande Railroad, terminating at Wolcott, which was a large terminus for wagons and stages.[16] North Park was served until 1913 by stage and freight wagons, while places like Craig and Steamboat Springs were provided with horse-drawn service. Craig, Lay, Maybell, Baggs, Dixon, Meeker, Axial, Rangely, and Vernal were all interconnected with stage routes. This was slow and costly service.

The promise of a new day came in 1903 when a railroad was proposed. It would begin in Denver, run through Middle Park, through the Gore Range, up the Yampa Valley, and into Steamboat Springs; from whence the line would go to Craig, then to Vernal, and finally terminate in Salt Lake City. When word of the route got out; all of northwestern Colorado was excited. Businessmen, cattlemen, miners, everyone saw the coming of a *railroad* as the answer to all of their problems.[17]

NOTES FOR CHAPTER 8

1. Henry E. Bender, *The Uintah Railway: The Gilsonite Route*, (Berkeley, Calif.: Howell-North, 1970), p. 16 and p. 21. See also: Richard A. Ronzio, "The Uintah Railway: The Gilsonite Road" in Denver Westerners *Brandbook* (Denver: Denver Westerners, 1959), p. 41. For a description of the environment of East Evacuation Creek see: E. Kinzie Gordon and Kris J. Kranzush, "Final Cultural Resource Inventory Report, 1978 Taiga/Coseka Drilling Program 1978 Northwest Pipeline Corporation West Foundation Creek Gathering System, Rio Blanco/Garfield Counties Colorado," (Boulder, Colo.: Gordon and Kranzush, 1979), Manuscript.

2. Ronzio, op. cit., p. 50.

3. Bender, op. cit., p. 57.

4. Ibid., p. 111.

5. Ibid., p. 185.

6. Ibid., p. 190.

7. Ibid., p. 191.

8. Ibid., p. 201.

9. Jackson County Library, Jackson County Scrapbook, Walden, Colorado, MSS in Colorado Historical Society, Denver, Colorado, n.d., unpaginated, 3 Volumes.

10. Frank R. Hallenback, *The Laramie Plains Line*, (Denver: Sage Books, 1960), p. 10. See also: *Laramie, Hahn's Peak and Pacific Railroad*, n.l.,n.p.,n.d.). This is a promotional pamphlet printed by the LHP&P in 1911 and contains many fine photographs of North Park in that year. Other sources include: Adah Bailey, *History of Jackson County, Colorado*, (Walden, Colo.: Jackson County *Star*, 1947) and Eva B. Mariette, "Memories of North Park," Xerox Scrapbook, MSS in Colorado Historical Society, Denver, Colorado n.d., unpaginated.

11. As related in Hallenback, op. cit., pp. 15-20.

12. Burroughs, *Steamboat*, op. cit., the author provides view of the area prior to 1917.

13. William Weston, *The Yampa Coal Fields of Routt County*, (Washington, D.C.: Government Printing Office, 1907), p. 4 and p. 29.

14. Ibid., pp. 29-30.

15. Nevin M. Fenneman, *The Yampa Coal Fields, Routt County, Colorado*, (Washington, D.C.: Government Printing Office, 1906).

16. *Historic American Building Survey, Bocco Residence, Wolcott, Colorado* (Prepared by F.J. Athearn, Bureau of Land Management, Denver, Colorado, April 1976), Repository: Library of Congress, Washington, D.C. Also: *E.E. Helm Interview*, CWA Interviews, Colorado Historical Society, Denver, Colorado.

17.   See: Thomas Tonge, *The "Moffat Road"*, (Denver: n.p., 1906).

Chapter 9

THE "MOFFAT ROAD" AND
NORTHWESTERN COLORADO

1903 - 1948

David Halliday Moffat came to Colorado in March 1860 from Omaha, Nebraska, penniless, having lost his fortune in a promotional scheme in that city.[1] Arriving in Denver, he worked among businessmen and miners, soon finding a need for banking in the newly created city.

David Moffat's Private Car *Marcia*, in Craig, 1981
Photo by F.J.Athearn

In partnership with John Evans, Moffat founded the First National Bank of Denver. Nearly every railroad scheme from the Colorado Central to the Rio Grande involved Moffat. Moffat also became interested in mining to the extent that he had holdings in Caribou, Leadville, Central City, and other major mining centers in Colorado. From these ventures, Moffat amassed a fortune estimated at some $9 million by 1902.[2]

In his sixties, Moffat decided the final project of his career would be building a standard gauge railroad directly through the Rocky Mountains, across the northwestern corner of the state, and on to Salt Lake City. Construction began in 1903 with a grade built up Coal Creek Canyon. Upon reaching the Continental Divide, Moffat had to make a decision; either build a major tunnel (about three miles long) through the mountains near Rollinsville at an estimated cost of $7,000,000, which would exhaust his fortune and end the railroad, or he could go over the Divide and conserve his resources. He chose the latter course. In doing so, Moffat built over Rollins Pass (the old Rollins Pass Freight Road) and down to Middle Park. The Denver Northwestern and Pacific, reached the Park in 1905, and for the first time cheap transportation was available.[3] The citizens of Kremmling, Hot Sulphur Springs, Fraser, Granby, and Grand Lake were delirious at the road's arrival.

91

However, such joy was short-lived when the road ran into financial difficulties.

When the railroad reached Hot Sulphur Springs, Moffat found he needed more money. He appealed to his friends in Denver who, while sympathetic, could not help him. He needed some $100 million in fresh capital. Moffat then went to New York where he tried to raise cash. This effort was unsuccessful. With eastern capital shut off, Moffat tried to get Belgian investors involved, but to no avail. The Moffat Road was stopped at Hot Sulphur Springs in 1907, and the long-sought Yampa coal fields were still fifty miles distant.[4] Moffat managed to raise enough money to continue construction through Gore Canyon into Egeria Park, up the Yampa Valley, and on to Oak Creek where the first real revenues for the road were finally tapped. Coal began to flow eastward toward Denver and the road seemed financially safer. The line was then extended north to Steamboat Springs, arriving at that city in 1909. The citizens of the town flocked to the outskirts of Steamboat where they swarmed over the first train to use the new tracks. A brass band played patriotic tunes, and the residents gave the railroad its station.[5]

The Craig, Colorado Depot is Typical of the
"Moffat Road's" Architecture, *Photo by F.J. Athearn*

Steamboat Springs became the terminus of the Denver, Northwestern, and Pacific, for at this point the railroad ran out of money. It cost $12,544,573.55 to get to Steamboat Springs, and Moffat exhausted all of his resources. He died in 1911, penniless, and with a railroad that went nowhere. The newly developing Yampa coal fields were the only potential sources of revenue for the road.

Kremmling, Colorado, about 1905
USGS Photo

In 1913 Newman Erb, a well-known railroad executive from the east, became General Manager of the reincorporated Denver and Salt Lake Railroad. Under his leadership the Moffat Road was able to keep rolling. In fact, Erb extended the mainline to Craig, Colorado, arriving at that town in 1913. While it was a valiant effort at extension, the Craig line could not save the road. The only benefit was that the Yampa Valley was served by rail, and Craig became a new cattle shipping center.

The D & SL was saved by World War I. By August 1917, the road had gone into receivership, and things were so bad that in January 1918, employees walked off their jobs, refusing to return until back wages were paid.[6] However, the war and demands for Yampa Valley coal kept the railroad alive until 1919. Revenues were high, and the wartime United States Railway Administration (a board that "nationalized" United States railways) pumped millions of dollars into the dying Moffat road.[7]

In 1921 the railroad applied for abandonment but it was refused, mostly due to the outcries of northwestern Colorado's population. The Denver and Salt Lake remained in bankruptcy.

Dotsero Cutoff Dedication, June 16, 1934
Colorado State Historical Society

There were many reasons for the poor condition of the road: the most important factor was that coal revenues never met expenses. Additionally, cattlemen soon found that shipping to Denver was dangerous, for cattle died along the way from the cold and poor service. The most serious problem faced by the Moffat Road was Rollins Pass; at 11,660 feet, it was one of the most difficult railway passes in the world, and during the winter it was virtually impossible to keep open. The Rollins Pass route caused cattle kills (in stock cars), accidents, passengers stranded for days on end, and any number of other problems. Middle Parkers were continually called to help dig out stranded trains. It was clear that Rollins Pass had to be eliminated.

The idea of a tunnel was hardly new. However, it was considered too expensive to blast through the Rockies. A tunnel bond issue occurred in 1919 but it was narrowly defeated by Colorado's voters. This seemed to end demands for a rail tunnel. The great Pueblo flood of 1921 stimulated new interest in a tunnel. Flood control was needed and supporters maintained that a diversion tunnel could help in this effort. Further, water from the Colorado River was necessary to keep Denver alive; hence, the citizens in that city were convinced that a combination rail and water tunnel was vital.[8] In 1922 a new bond issue was floated to the sum of $9,000,000 and this time it passed. The Moffat Tunnel was authorized and the western slope "boomed" again.

Construction on the Moffat Tunnel began in 1923, with a camp built at East Portal, Colorado. From there, the Rockies were penetrated. It took four years and over $40,000,000 to blast a six-mile tunnel to carry both water and rail traffic. The Moffat Tunnel provided more direct, and certainly more reliable, transportation into the northwest corner of the state.[9]

The Denver and Salt Lake Railroad, despite having little invested in the Moffat Tunnel, was still in serious trouble. During the 1920s, its trackage was leased by the Denver and Rio Grande Western Railroad. Service into Craig continued, but not nearly on the scale that was projected. In 1931 the Denver and Rio Grande got permission to build the Dotsero Cutoff, running from Bond (Orestod), Colorado, to the Rio Grande's mainline (Dotsero) at the mouth of Glenwood Canyon. This shortcut eliminated 181 miles and the Rio Grande had a direct mainline through the mountains from Denver to Salt Lake City. The line to Craig became a branch service line and northwestern Colorado languished once again.[10]

One of the most interesting factors in the coming of a railroad to northwestern Colorado was the excitement that occurred. As was typical in Colorado, the promise of opening the corner caused a "boom." From 1906 until the late 1920s, continual efforts were made to promote the region.

Thomas Tonge, a Denver promoter, wrote in 1906 that "the Yampa and White Rivers in northwestern Colorado have as yet only been very partially utilized for irrigation purposes, but with the advent of the Moffat Road, now being built from Denver to Salt Lake City, and the settling up of the tributary country, irrigation systems will be constructed."[11] Clearly, Tonge tried to promote agriculture in the area. He provided statistics that showed a great potential for the corner, while at the same time pointing out that only the railroad could make development possible.[12] The Denver, Northwestern, and Pacific hired eminent geologist, R.D. George, to study the coal fields of the Yampa Valley and Moffat County. George concluded that there were minerals such as coal, clay, copper, carnotite (uranium), asphaltic sands, gold, gypsum, iron, oil and gas throughout the region, and all that was needed was transportation.[13] Naturally, the railroad was delighted to use such information for its promotions. A series of USGS reports were published between 1915 and 1925 that were used to help assess the region.[14] The USGS made a careful study of the land and concluded that there was great potential, but little transportation.

Another "boom" took place when the Moffat Tunnel was proposed.[15] The citizens of the Yampa Valley saw a bore as the answer to all their problems. For with a tunnel, the line to Salt Lake would be completed.

With this in mind, Steamboat Springs, led by Charles Leckenby, began a promotional campaign to lure people into the valley. A booklet entitled, "An Imperial Empire: Northwestern Colorado" described the area as having major mining at Oak Creek, an oil gusher at Hamilton, and head lettuce being raised in the upper Yampa Valley and Granby areas. The town of Oak Creek was cited as being so progressive that it had a soft drink bottling plant, a cigar factory, and a packing house, not to mention a saw mill and creamery.[16] It was noted that Kremmling had a new high school, and that Granby

95

was a serious agricultural area.

In 1925 the Moffat Tunnel league was founded to "boom" the region. Not only was the tunnel considered important, but so was the commercial promotion of the Yampa Valley. The same year the League put out a "Resource Edition" of the Moffat Tunnel District Development Association's publication. In it the dairy, oil, cattle, sheep, lettuce, and mineral industries were heavily promoted.[17] The next year's "Resource Edition" pushed most of the same things that the 1925 edition had "boomed;" even Oak Creek put out a "Centennial Issue" that was a copy of the 1926 "Resource Edition."[18]

Other towns got into the act earlier as witnessed in 1912, when the town of Hayden published a booklet touting that city as the "center of northwest Colorado." Agriculture, mining, and cattle raising were said to be the major industries, and Hayden could provide all necessary services. The Moffat Road, said the city, would provide the critical transportation.

As usual, the intensive promotion of the region did little good, for while agriculture remained stable, the lettuce industry died and the coal "boom" gave out - causing towns like Phippsburg, Oak Creek, and Yampa to lose considerable population. The Upper Yampa Valley fell into deep depression during the 1920s, 1930s, and 1940s.

One benefit of the Moffat Road was that subsidiary industries developed to help supply construction crews. Towns like Fraser, Tabernash, Granby, Kremmling, Hot Sulphur Springs, and the Upper Yampa Valley towns became supply centers, by and large gaining their present population at this time. An example of this was the development of a timber industry in Middle Park. Several companies were formed to provide bridge timbers, ties, and other needs for the railroad. Charles Wolcott, in 1905, founded the Rocky Mountain Lumber Company. It was capitalized at $100,000 and the town of Monarch, Colorado, came of the company. Also in 1905 the Rocky Mountain Railway Company was incorporated to carry lumber from Granby to Monarch, a distance of 16 miles.[19]

After the railroad went through and into the Yampa Valley, the lumber business gave out in Middle Park. In 1908 Rocky Mountain Lumber went out of business after a fire destroyed the mill and box factory at Monarch. The fate of most other lumber companies in Middle Park was as dismal.[20] The supply towns tended to languish, but never entirely faded away. Land development did take place and it seemed as if the region would develop, but this was only a dream.

NOTES FOR CHAPTER 9

1. Lyle Dorsett, *The Queen City - A History of Denver.* (Boulder, Colo: Pruett, 1977), p. 16.

2. See: Edgar C. McMechen, *The Moffat Tunnel of Colorado,* (Denver: Wahlgren, 1927), 2 Vols.; Edward T. Bollinger, *Rails That Climb: The Story of the Moffat Road,* (Golden, Colo.: Colorado Railroad Museum, 1979), Edward T. Bollinger and Frederick Bauer, *The Moffat Road,* (Chicago: Swallow Press, 1962), and Harold Boner, *The Giant's Ladder: David H. Moffat and His Railroad,* (Milwaukee: Kalmbach, 1962).

3. Boner, op. cit., p. 77.

4. Bollinger, op. cit., p. 309 and Boner, Ibid., p. 137.

5. Burroughs, *Steamboat,* op. cit., p. 180.

6. Bollinger, op. cit., p. 309.

7. Boner, op. cit., p. 167 and p. 176.

8. Ibid., p. 176 and p. 181.

9. McMechen, op. cit., p. 127 and p. 161. Vol. 1.

10. Ibid., p. 180.

11. Boner, op. cit., p. 195 and p. 201.

12. Thomas Tonge, *Handbook of Colorado Resources,* (Denver: Smith-Brooks, 1907), pp. 15-16.

13. Ibid., p. 20.

14. R. D. George, *The Denver and Salt Lake Railroad: Coal Oil Shale and Hydrocarbons,* (Denver: n.p., 11918) pp. 8-26.

15. See Hoyt S. Gale, *Coal Fields of Northwestern Colorado and Northwestern Utah,* (Washington: Government Printing Office 1910); E. G. Woodruff, *Oil Shale of Northwestern Colorado and Northeastern Utah,* (Washington: Government Printing Office, 1914): A. L. Beekly, *Geology and Coal Resources of North Park, Colorado,* (Washington: Government Printing Office, 1915); Dean E. Winchester, *Oil Shale in Northwestern Colorado and Adjacent Areas,* (Washington: Government Printing Office, 1916); Marius R. Campbell, *The Twenty Mile Park District of the Yampa Coal Field, Routt County, Colorado,* (Washington: Government Printing Office, 1923); and E. T. Hancock, *Geology and Coal Resources of the Axial and Monument Butte Quadrangles, Moffat County, Colorado.* Washington: Government Printing Office, 1925).

16. Federated Commercial Clubs of Northwestern Colorado, "An Imperial Empire: Northwestern Colorado," June, 1924, Steamboat *Pilot,* Steamboat Springs, Colorado.

17. See: Moffat Tunnel District Development Association, "Resource Edition," (Steamboat Springs, Colorado: Steamboat Pilot, 1926), Moffat Tunnel League, "Resource Edition," (Steamboat Springs, Colorado: Steamboat *Pilot,* 1927).

18. Oak Creek *Times,* "Centennial Edition," Volume 18, Number 23, March 25, 1926.

19. See: Frank Wolcott, "Monarch of Grand County," *Westerners Brandbook,* (Denver, 1954).

20. Ibid., p. 152.

Chapter 10

MODERN DEVELOPMENT

OF NORTHWESTERN COLORADO

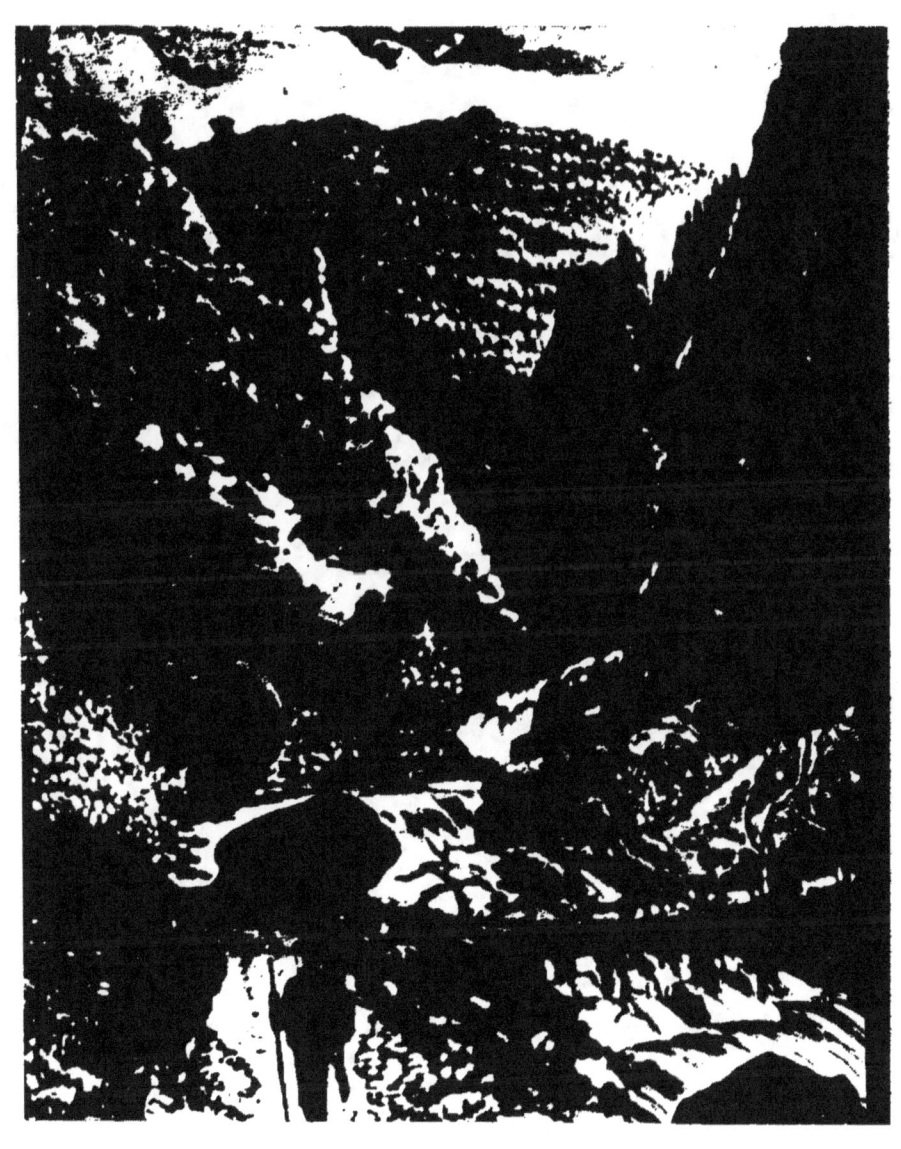

1890 - 1980

The most recent stages of development in northwestern Colorado came over a ninety-year period. From 1890 to 1980 towns were founded; natural resources were developed, and vast areas of the public domain were withdrawn from use by homesteaders and cattlemen. The period was one of consolidation and reorganization; the old frontier rule of "he who got there first" was no longer in effect. Now settlers had to deal with large corporations, governmental agencies, and the law.

After the Ute removal in 1880, townsite companies organized towns within northwestern Colorado in anticipation of the rush that would come. Additionally, better transportation routes from Wyoming helped stir interest in settlement. In 1882 the town of Rangely was founded, replacing the older town of Golden City, that was located at the mouth of Cottonwood Creek. Steamboat Springs, as mentioned, was founded in 1885 by James Crawford, while in 1889 the Craig Land and Mercantile Company was formed. That year 320 acres were purchased from Frank Ranney by Frank Russell, Jerry Hill, and Reverend W. B. Craig for $2,500. Additionally, a Mr. Barkley sold 160 acres to the company for $1,500.[1] W. H. Tucker, a partner, laid out the streets, and in 1892 a hotel was erected. The general store at Hayden was bought out and moved to Craig; it was subsequently sold to the Hugus system in 1893 or 1894. The Craig townsite was obviously designed to make a profit for its founders. But the town grew slowly and it was hardly a money making operation. As one old timer put it: "Nobody got rich out of the Craig Company."[2]

Another example of townbuilding was the creation of Hayden, Colorado, in 1894 when this townsite was platted by William Walker. Prior to this, Hayden was a little trading post catering to first the Indians, and later, cattlemen. Walker's townsite company proposed to develop and sell property, and in 1906 the town was incorporated. It was the fourth or fifth largest city in the Yampa River Valley.[3]

Hayden was built to compete with Craig as the "capital" of the northwest. The two towns fought each other for trade and other services for cattlemen in the area. Steamboat Springs, being somewhat isolated near the Park Range, remained a supply point for the eastern sectors.

In 1912 Hahn's Peak finally lost its status as Routt County seat. A fire in 1910 wiped out most of the town and, under considerable pressure, the seat was moved to Steamboat Springs. Craig, Hayden, Meeker, Axial, Maybell, and Lay were all in the competition.[4]

Blevin's Placer Dredge on Lay Creek, about 8 Miles
North of Lay, *Photo by H.S. Gale, USGS*

Craig got its way in 1914 when Moffat County was carved from Routt, and that city became the seat of the new county, much to the dismay of Hayden, the other contender.[5]

One of the more interesting economic features in the region was the J. W. Hugus chain of stores. These businesses were located at Meeker (headquarters), Craig, Hayden, Palisade, Clifton, Rifle, Wolcott, Axial, Pagoda, Walden, Granby, Steamboat Springs, Rawlins, and Wamsutter.[6] The chain operated general stores throughout the region, serving cattlemen, miners, and settlers alike. The Hugus chain, incorporated in 1889, was the largest single corporation in northwestern Colorado. It had seven auxiliary banks and owned the Wyoming Transportation Company, that acted as freight service for the Hugus stores while providing stage and freight lines throughout western Colorado.[7] The Hugus chain folded in the 1930s, a victim of the depression, but the company was well-remembered, for it helped many struggling settlers or cattlemen survive. It was said of the Hugus chain: "They were almost the backbone of this country. They gave unlimited credit to the farmers..."[8]

Meeker was also the home of the Harp Transportation Company founded in 1887. At first, the company was a stage line run by Simp Harp of Meeker between that city and New Castle, Colorado. The Harp, Wright, and Daum Stage Company sold out to "Kit" Carson (no relation to the well-known Christopher "Kit" Carson of mountain and political fame) in 1888 and he started running stages from Glenwood Springs to Meeker. However, the Carson Stage Line was so unrealiable that it soon went broke.[9] Simp Harp began a new stage company that ran to Rifle, and continued to serve Meeker by stage until 1915, when Harp bought a Cadillac motor car that he used for service. The Harp Company continues to serve the White River Valley and western Colorado and is the oldest continuous nonrail transportation company in the state of Colorado.[10]

As early as 1880 a deer and elk meat industry developed in North Park. One pioneer family, the Rhea's of North Park, provided over 2,000 pounds of dried elk and deer meat for Denver and Cheyenne butchers. At the same time, a major elk industry operated in the Meeker area.[11] Here, thousands of pounds of elk meat was shipped during the late 1880s and early 1890s to Denver, Cheyenne, and points east. This business died prior to 1900 because the slaughter of elk so depleted the herds that areas once swarming with the animals were no longer profitable for hunting.[12]

Another early industry of the region that has continued to grow was the hunting and fishing business. For many years elk, deer, antelope, and other game animals were hunted. However, the region got national publicity in 1901 when Vice President Theodore Roosevelt came to Meeker and hunted in the nearby Flat Top Mountains, bagging a mountain lion. The Roosevelt visit provided the stimulus and publicity needed for the creation of a hunting industry. Trapper's Lake, the Flattop Mountains, and other places such as the Elk River Valley were promoted as excellent hunting areas.[13]

In addition to development of land in the region, the United States government began efforts at resource protection. As noted, the White River Forest Reserve was withdrawn in 1891, and became the White River National Forest in 1905. Other forest areas were withdrawn in line with national policy; Routt National Forest (1905) and Arapaho National Forest (1906) were created. With the withdrawal of millions of acres of grazing and forest lands, the government became, to a large extent, the arbiter of disputes between cattlemen and sheepmen, settlers and miners, and others. With the formation of these protected reserves, early Forest Rangers who patrolled them became symbols of continuing efforts at conservation. It took a number of years for most farmers and cattlemen to accept grazing permits. The days of the "old frontier" were gone in the northwestern regions by 1920.[14]

Additionally, thanks to the furor stirred up by antiquity robbing in the southwest, mainly in the Mesa Verde and Chaco Canyon regions, the Antiquities Act of 1906 was passed to protect ancient historic sites.[15] Out of this Act came development of a National Monument System to provide protection for historic, scenic, or archeologically valuable sites. One such area in northwest Colorado were the highly scenic canyons of the Green and Yampa Rivers, about which John Wesley Powell was so enthusiastic. Bones of dinosaurs were found in the Utah canyons and to protect these antiquities, an area of the rivers was formed as Dinosaur National Monument in 1915. This withdrew the lands in and around the canyons and provided protection from exploitation by unscrupulous developers. In 1938 the Monument was expanded into far western Colorado and enlarged to 326 square miles.[16]

103

At the same time, Enos Mills, longtime resident of Estes Park, Colorado and a well-known naturalist, campaigned for the creation of a national park and wildlife area near Estes Park. In 1915 Rocky Mountain National Park was decreed and thousands of acres on both sides of the Continental Divide were made national tourist attractions. During the 1920s, Fall River Road was built to provide a highway from Estes Park to Grand Lake, Colorado, and soon thousands of tourists were using the spectacular drive. Rocky Mountain Park drew tourists into Middle Park (reminiscent of an earlier day) and later into the far northwestern corner of the state.[17]

One of the other "discoveries" in northwest Colorado was that of oil. Oil was known about quite early; in 1893 oil springs were found on Oil Creek, and the next year a company was organized to develop the seeps. Nothing seems to have come of this effort, for no major oil production took place until 1902. In 1902 the Poole well was brought in near Rangely, and an oil boom ensued. It was short-lived because deep wells had to be developed to tap reserves, and for the amount of oil gained it was not worth the effort.[18] The Rangely fields continued to produce on a modest basis and were superseded in the early 1920s, when a number of basins were tapped for the first time. In 1924 the Iles field was brought in, while in 1926 Hiawatha began to produce. Powder Wash proved out in 1931, while the Thornburgh field has been producing since 1925. Tow Creek, one of the earlier fields, came in during 1924 and Rangely produced on a modest scale from 1890.[19] Since these early fields were discovered, numerous other oil fields were found and worked. The real boom came during and after World War II when oil demand skyrocketed.

North Park oil was discovered and later developed during the 1920s. The Colorado Immigration Board noted that in northwestern Colorado there were numerous oil domes

Requina Oil Well Number 1, Rio Blanco County,
No Date, *Photo by H.S. Gale, USGS*

such as the Moffat, Iles, Gossard, Elk Springs, Snake River, Thornburg, Axial, Beaver Creek, Sage Creek, Tow Creek, Deep Creek, and Wilson Creek.[20] Yet, with all this potential, production remained low. For example, the Hiawatha field, to date, has produced only 129,296 barrels, while Powder Wash produced 927,738 barrels and the Iles field has produced 357,753 barrels.[21] Nevertheless, there were a few good producers such as the Moffat field, which produced 5,444,849 barrels since 1925.[22]

One of the last major developments in the northwest was an attempt at homestead

Great Divide Post Office, 1981
Photo by F.J. Athearn

colonization. In 1915 the Great Divide Homestead Colony Number One was organized to attempt dryland farming near the present-day Great Divide. Volney T. Hoggatt, bodyguard of Frederick G. Bonfils, founder of the Denver *Post* promoted this scheme. Hoggatt became editor of a magazine dedicated to dryland farming named *Great Divide*. It was published by the Denver *Post*, and was a mouthpiece for Hoggatt's schemes. Hoggatt also had the advantage of being the registrar of the State Land Board. He was appointed to that post in 1912. The idea of colonization was not unique for as early as 1911, the Great Northern Irrigation and Power Company contracted with the state of Colorado to reclaim some 150,000 acres of land. The company failed to hold up its end of the bargain and went under.[23] Here is where Hoggatt used his position in state office to secure about 275,000 acres of land northwest of Craig including some of the Great Northern's. In March 1916 a trainload of immigrants arrived with "fifteen carloads of household goods and stock and one coach containing sixty men, women, and children."[24] Craig saw a new boom coming, and noted that there was simply no room for the hundreds of settlers expected.[25] By 1917 hundreds of miles of barbed wire was strung, and water wells had been drilled;

Great Divide Colony Number One, Ca. 1918
Colorado State Historical Society

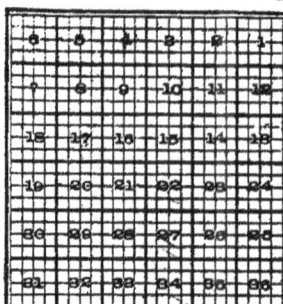
Hoggatt's Great Divide colony was in full operation. The initial success of this venture stimulated a proposed colony in Carbon County, Wyoming, that luckily never came about. The colony survived until the mid-1930s with indifferent success. Hoggatt continually

promoted the effort through the *Denver Post*, until his death in 1934.[26] There is no estimate of the number of settlers who arrived in the area, but considering the land and lack of water, some settlers departed as fast as they came. For Craig, the land boom never amounted to much, and the economy of the region gained little from the experience. The Great Divide adventure proved once again that "booms" were not the answer for northwestern Colorado; it is a good example of unwise land use in the West.

In the years following World War I, the Ku Klux Klan arose once more. While its strength lay mainly in the industrial cities of the middle west, Colorado was a breeding ground for this disease. In fact, in 1924 C. J. Morley, a Klansman was placed in the Governor's Mansion for two years. The Klan was seen in northwestern Colorado, particularly at Steamboat Springs where it was well-organized. That there was a substantial membership was evidenced by the numbers of sheets and pillowcases hung out to dry in the weekly laundry. The Klan died out during the late 1920s as the nation's economy boomed and has not revived, to any extent, in recent times.[27]

Within the last fifty years, this region has been underdeveloped and newer industries such as hunting, fishing, and skiing have helped take up the slack. One of the more significant events in the area was the advent of the automobile and paved roads. In the early 1920s Berthoud, Loveland, and Fall River passes were paved, providing easy access to the parks. Beyond Middle and North Parks, roads were extended over the Gore Range and into the Yampa Valley. The coal industry helped bring roads into the Upper Yampa Valley, while ranchers were served by new roads from Wyoming south. Looking at modern roadmaps, one sees a single major road from Craig to Wyoming, and only one leading south into the White River country. A highway was built along the White River to Rangely and on to Utah. The major east-west connection was U.S. 40, that was built across the West as the "Victory Highway" in the early 1920s in order to provide a transcontinental roadway. This highway crossed the entire region and provided a backbone for the current road system.[28] The automobile provided cheap and easy transportation for the nation, yet the northwest corner, while greatly benefited by the car, remained isolated. The coming of cars and trucks certainly helped lower transportation costs, bring tourists into the area, and provide easier local movement; but the impact, as with the coming of the railroad, turned out to be rather limited.

One of the new industries that began in the 1920s and has been greatly stimulated by automobiles was skiing. Skiing clubs sprang up in Middle Park by 1921, while Steamboat Springs discovered the sport in the mid-1920s. From these small beginnings, the industry struggled along on a local basis until after World War II, when an increase in Colorado's population helped development of ski resorts. Automobile travel into the mountains became easier and soon the Front Range was covered with ski areas.[29]

Since 1940, the northwestern corner of Colorado has seen a period of little growth followed by a major energy boom. World War II brought about a revival of agriculture, particularly wheat and cattle. Dryland farming in the Great Divide region was consolidated when many homesteaders went out of business. The Depression of the 1930s caused marginal agricultural enterprises to fail, mostly small cattlemen and dryland farmers.

The severity of the Depression coupled with unprecedented drought brought an end to marginal subsistence farming throughout the west. Landholdings were consolidated into much larger masses and thus became economically workable. Additionally, the Bankhead-Jones Land Utilization Act provided for repurchase, by the U.S. Government, of marginal farm lands in drought regions. A number of homesteads in Great Divide were sold to the government from 1938 to 1941 under Bankhead-Jones and these lands (ranging from 320 to 640-acre parcels) fell to the management of the General Land Office, which later became BLM. Other LU Repurchase lands in the west were primarily on the eastern plains of Colorado, Kansas, Nebraska, South Dakota, and Texas.[30] These lands became National Grasslands administered by the U.S. Forest Service.

The war also temporarily stimulated coal production in the Upper Yampa Valley. The mines of Oak Creek, Phippsburg, Mount Harris, and other coal towns were reopened and produced vital coal supplies for the war effort. Equally, the bankrupt Moffat Road gained revenues for its lessee, the Rio Grande.[31] The oil and gas fields of Rangely also benefited from increased wartime production, for oil supplies were badly needed by the Allies, and Rangely was worked at full capacity. This trend continued well into the 1950s and has depleted the fields.

The coal, wheat, cattle, and oil booms were short and when World War II ended, so did prosperity. By 1948 mines around Steamboat Springs and Hayden were closing. The Mount Harris open pit mine was abandoned at this time. Oak Creek fell into depression once more as coal prices plummeted. The Moffat Road, once the pride of northwest Colorado, was sold to the Denver and Rio Grande Western in 1947 and the Denver and Salt Lake was merged into the Rio Grande at that time, never to regain its corporate identity.[32]

About the only area in the region that sustained war growth was Rangely where ever-increasing demands for oil and natural gas caused the town to grow. So great was its increase that in the early 1950s Northwestern Community College was built at Rangely and it has served as a junior college ever since.

As was common throughout Colorado's western slope during the late 1940s and early 1950s, a uranium "boom" occurred near Maybell, where strip mines were developed to extract uranium ores close to the surface. The mines were not profitable and were abandoned by 1960. However, their evidences are still seen by gapping, ugly holes left in the earth.

108

Steamboat Springs profited from an increasing skiing demand; south of town, the Mount Werner (Storm Mountain) Ski Area developed in the early 1960s and Steamboat Springs became known as a world-class ski resort. The major event that vaulted Steamboat into the "big leagues" was the purchase of its ski area by LTV Corporation which put millions of dollars into the mountain.

Middle and North Parks changed very little during the 1940s and 1950s. Cattle and timber sustained the parks although oil in North Park continued to be pumped and some coal was mined near Hebron. But the operations were small. Perhaps one of the main changes in Middle Park was the "discovery," by tourists, of Winter Park. This ski resort was built by the Denver Water Department in the 1930s as part of Denver's transmountain diversion projects (Moffat Tunnel). It was, and is, the largest municipally-owned ski area in America. The Rio Grande Railroad was responsible, in large part, for Winter Park's popularity, for in 1948 the railroad began a Denver to Salt Lake City service with the new, streamlined, Vista-Dome *California Zephyr*, considered by many at the time, the finest train in the United States. Thousands of tourists viewed the beauty of Middle Park from Dome cars, and many returned in the winter to ski. The *Zephyr* stopped at Winter Park and Granby and provided an easy access to Rocky Mountain National Park.[33]

The Rio Grande *Zephyr* in the Colorado River Canyon, on the old "Moffat Road", 1981, *Photo by F.J. Athearn*

Craig lost its passenger rail service in 1967 when the Rio Grande canceled the *Yampa Valley Mail*, a train that had served northwest Colorado since 1913. However, this loss was overcome by air service, with Frontier Airlines serving Hayden, Rocky Mountain Airways flying into Steamboat Springs and later Craig. Rocky Mountain pulled out of Craig in 1979, but was replaced by the now defunct Star Airways. Frontier and Rocky Mountain continued to provide northwest Colorado with its only commercial air transportation system.

The rest of the northwest corner was not so lucky with tourists. Highway 40, while providing some trade, was not a major access route for tourists, except for the visitors going to Dinosaur Monument and those on their way to Salt Lake City. Craig had U.S. 40 running through the middle of town, and there were no stoplights. In fact, U.S. 40 users could probably brag that there were no lights between Denver and Salt Lake City.

From 1950 to about 1970, Craig, Steamboat, Meeker, Rangely, and the northwest generally saw little change. Cattle, sheep, wheat, and some tourism sustained the economy and provided a living. There was virtually no growth and the corner remained a backwater in Colorado. But this was soon to change.

Shadow Mountain Trailer Court, Craig, Colorado, 1981
Photo by F.J. Athearn

In the late 1960s an ever increasing demand for electrical power caused utilities to consider building new generating plants. Most cities did not want the pollution of coal-fired generators near them and to save transportation costs, power companies decided to build plants near the source of fuel and well away from population centers.

In Colorado, one of the greatest sources of coal lay near Hayden and Steamboat Springs. In September 1976, Colorado-Ute Electric Association began operation of a generation plant near Hayden, Colorado, and that started the present-day energy boom.[34] Coal mines that had lain inactive since the 1940s were reopened. The Edna Mine near Oak Creek began stripping coal, while at Hayden, strip mines to feed the plant were built.

Colorado-Ute proceeded to build a new generation facility at Craig and opened the Trapper Mine to feed the hungry boilers. As coal-fired generation plants were built on the eastern slope of Colorado, coal demands soared and soon the coal fields of northwestern Colorado were booming. By 1978, Energy Fuels' Mines were producing five-unit trains of coal a day to fire Public Service's plants in Denver.[35] Unit trains rumbled down the Rio Grande from Oak Creek to Denver many times a day. Powerful engines dragged hundred car trains over the old "Moffat Road" and what was once the orphan of the railroad has become its primary revenue producer.[36]

Not only did coal mines open in the Hayden/Oak Creek area, but near Axial a two million-ton-a-year facility operated by W. R. Grace was put into production in the late 1970s. To remove the mineral, a new railroad line was built from Craig to Axial, a distance of some 30 miles.[37]

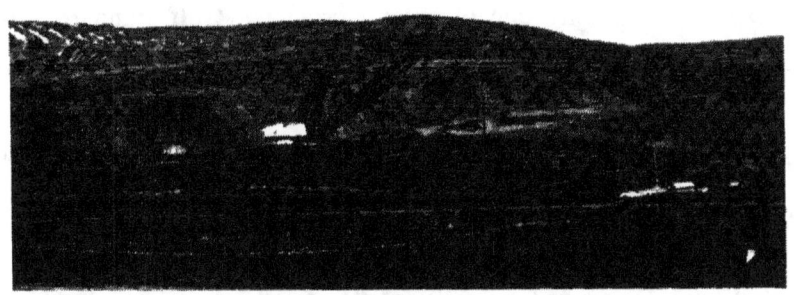

Energy Fuels Mine Dragline near Hayden, Colorado, 1980
Photo by F.J. Athearn

With the rip-roaring mining and construction in and around Craig, the town dramatically increased in size and population. To handle the construction workers on the Craig power plant, a trailer court west of Craig was built. Hayden saw a sizeable increase in population, complete with attendant mobile home parks. Craig's population jumped from 4,205 in 1970 to 7,715 in 1978.[38] As with any such growth, Craig has suffered from the social strains of a "boomtown" economy. Suicides, alcholism, divorce and murder are up. But this is only natural when one societal structure is overlain by a new one. The "cowboys versus the miners" conflicts are there, but considering the tensions, Craig and Hayden are remarkably well-adjusted towns. Northwestern Colorado has never seen a boom like this and energy development seems assured for the next twenty years. The question now is, how much more coal will be developed. The Department of the Interior is projecting regional coal development of over 500 million tons during a twenty-year period.[39]

Craig was not the only area to be impacted by energy development. As noted, Rangely produced oil from 1900 on. Heavy pumping has diminished the fields and tertiary recovery methods such as steam injection are now being used to enhance production. Despite the declining Rangely fields, natural gas development is steadily increasing. Baxter Pass and Douglas Canyon are two major gas fields and hundreds of wells have been drilled in these areas.

The ground that Dominguez and Escalante once trod in Douglas Canyon is a maze of wells, gathering lines, and transportation pipelines. The northern end of the canyon was listed as the Canyon Pintado Historic District in 1974.[40]

111

Meeker too has seen considerable development. Once a small cattle and tourist town, Meeker has grown from 1,597 people in 1970 to 2,976 in 1978. Much of the growth is due to oil shale development in the Piceance Basin. Occidental Petroleum's Tract Cb oil shale mine is being built and will represent an *in situ* (on site) shale processing facility, that, when completed, will be a full production shale plant. The head works of the mine shaft rise hundreds of feet above the Piceance and it seems that the old dream of shale is about to be fulfilled. But Occidental is only one of several projects. Gulf-Standard is working on its Tract Ca plant, while the Superior Oil Company has proposed a multi-mineral mine at the juncture of Piceance Creek and the White River.[41] Oil shale, while maybe not fully feasible yet, promises to be a serious entry in the energy field and northwestern Colorado will be the proving grounds.

While energy development is the most active and economically important factor in modern-day northwest Colorado, the cattle and farming industries not only still survive but are doing rather well. Wheat prices in the middle 1970s made dryland wheat highly profitable and many acres of land were planted. Equally as cattle and sheep prices rose, livestock growers increased their herds. As always, farming is dependent on supply and demand, and with fluctuations of the national economy, local farmers' fortunes are tied to the nation.

The northwestern corner, today, is showing signs of fulfilling the dreams that it harbored for over a hundred years. All the things that were needed to foster growth and development are finally in place, and with energy a national priority, there is little reason to believe that this region will not grow and prosper for many years. However, the most important question that remains unasked is at what price?

NOTES FOR CHAPTER 10

1. CWA Interviews, Moffat County, 1933-34, MSS, in Colorado Historical Society, Denver, Colorado, Pamphlet 356.

2. Ibid., 1933-34.

3. Hayden High School, "Early History of Routt County," MS, Hayden, Colorado, 1925, p. 3.

4. Ibid., p. 10.

5. CWA Interview, op. cit., Pamphlet 356.

6. CWA Interviews, Rio Blanco County, 1933-34, MSS in Colorado Historical Society, Denver, Colorado.

7. Ibid., 1933-34.

8. Ibid., 1933-34.

9. Meeker *Herald,* 1888.

10. CWA Interviews, Rio Blanco, op. cit. 1933, Document 108.

11. U.S. Forest Service, "History of the Routt Forest," MS, in Routt Forest Ranger Station, Steamboat Springs, Colorado. 1972. p. 242.

12. CWA Interviews, Rio Blanco, op. cit., 1933.

13. Ibid., 1933-34.

14. Ibid., 1933-34.

15. See: Ronald F. Lee, *The Antiquities Act of 1906,* (Washington, D.C.: National Park Service, 1970).

16. See: Wallace Stegner, *This is Dinosaur,* (New York, Knopf, 1955).

17. See: Enos A. Mills, *The Rocky Mountain National Park,* (Estes Park, Colo.: n.p., 1932).

18. CWA Interviews, op. cit., 1933-34. See also: *State of Colorado, Oil and Gas Conservation Commission, Oil and Gas Statistics, 1974,* (Denver: State of Colorado, 1975), p. 141.

19. *Oil and Gas Statistics,* op. cit., pp. 132-145.

20. Colorado State Board of Immigration, *Colorado Mineral, Oil and Shale Resources,* (Denver: n.p., 1925), pp. 25-30.

21. *Oil and Gas Statistics,* op. cit., pp. 65-67.

22. Ibid., p. 66. 23.

23. Burroughs, *Where the Old West Stayed Young,* op. cit., pp. 328-330.

24. Ibid., p. 332.

25. Interview, with Henry Grandt, Bureau of Land Management, Craig, Colorado, 1978. Also: Burroughs, *Where the Old West Stayed Young,* op. cit., p. 333.

26. Burroughs, op. cit., pp. 336-337.

27. "Early History of Routt County," op. cit., p. 21.

28. Burroughs, op. cit., *Steamboat,* p. 180.

29. See: Nell Pauly, Grand Lake: *Ghosts of the Shootin',* (Grand Lake, Colo.: n.p., 1961), p. 75 and Burroughs, *Steamboat,* op. cit., pp. 189-191.

30. Worster, op. cit.

31. Robert G. Athearn, *Rebel of the Rockies,* (New Haven: Yale University Press, 1962), p. 311.

32. Ibid., p. 325.

33. See: Karl R. Zimmerman, *CZ-The Story of the California Zephyr,* (Oradell, Calif.: Delford Press, 1972), and Athearn, op. cit., p. 331.

34. U.S. Department of the Interior, Bureau of Land Management, *Final Impact Statement, Northwest Colorado Coal,* (Denver: Bureau of Land Management, 1975), p. 10, Vol. I.

35. U.S. Department of the Interior, Bureau of Land Management, *Northwest Supplemental Report,* (Denver: Bureau of Land Management, 1978), p. I-19.

36. Rio Grande Industries, *Annual Report,* (Denver: Rio Grande, 1979).

37. USDI, BLM *Supplemental,* op. cit., p. I-18.

38. U.S. Department of the Interior, Bureau of Land Management, *Draft Green River-Hams Fork Regional Coal Environmental Impact Statement,* (Denver: Bureau of Land Management, 1980) Vol. I, p. 126.

39. USDI, BLM, Green River-Hams Fork, Vol. I, op. cit., pp. 85-97 and Philip L. Fradkin, "Craig, Colorado: Population unknown, elevation 6,185 feet", *Audobon,* July, 1977, Vol. 79, No. 4, p. 121.

40. *National Register of Historic Places*, "Canon Pintado Historic District," (Washington, D.C.: Keeper of the Register, 1973) and Gordon and Kranzush, op. cit.

41. USDI, BLM, *Green River-Hams Fork*, op. cit., p. 126, Vol. 1. See also U.S. Department of the Interior, Bureau of Land Management, *Draft Environmental Statement, Proposed Superior Oil Company Land Exchange and Oil Shale Resource Development*, (Denver: Bureau of Land Management, 1979).

BIBLIOGRAPHY

PRIMARY SOURCES

Manuscripts

Baldwin, Susan. "Historic Resource Study: Dutchtown and Lulu City, Rocky Mountain Mountain National Park, Colorado." Boulder, Colo.: Creative Land Use, 1980. MS at National Park Service, Denver, Colo.

Byers, William N. "A History of Colorado." n.d. MSS in Western History Collections, University of Colorado, Boulder, Colorado.

Civil Works Administration. (CWA), Interviews. 1933-34. MSS in Colorado Historical Society, Denver, Colorado. For: Routt, Moffat, Rio Blanco and Garfield Counties, Colorado.

Crawford, James H. Interview MSS. 1926. In Western History Collection, University of Colorado, Boulder, Colorado.

Cragin, F. W. Collection. MSS in Pioneer Museum, Colorado Springs, Colorado.

Crumine, Homer (Interviewer). Vic Hansen papers and interviews. n.d. In Western History Collection, University of Colorado, Boulder, Colorado.

Duchrow, Linda L. "Geologic History of Colorado." Typescript. University of Colorado at Denver, 1974.

Gordon, E. Kinzie and Kris J. Kranzush. "Final Cultural Resource Inventory Report, 1978 Taiga/Coseka Drilling Program, 1978 Northwest Pipeline Corporation West Foundation Creek Gathering System, Rio Blanco/Garfield Counties, Colorado." Boulder, Colo.: Gordon and Kranzush, 1979. MS at Bureau of Land Management, Craig, Colorado.

Hayden High School. "Early History of Routt County," 1925. MS in University of Colorado, Boulder, Colorado.

Historic American Building Survey. "Wolcott, Colorado Stage Station." Prepared by F. J. Athearn, Bureau of Land Management, 1976. In Library of Congress, HABS Collection, Washington, D.C.

Hoy, J. S. Collection. MS in Penrose Library, Colorado Springs, Colorado.

Jackson County Library. Scrapbook. MS in Colorado Historical Society, Denver, Colorado.

Jones, M. F. Statement. MS in Western History Collection, University of Colorado, Boulder, Colorado.

Londoner, Wolfe. "Colorado Mining Camps." 1886. MS in Western History Collections, University of Colorado, Boulder, Colorado.

Mariette, Eva B. "Memories of North Park." 1969. MS in Western History Collection, University of Colorado, Boulder, Colorado.

Moffat Tunnel League. Papers. MS in Denver Public Library, Denver, Colorado.

National Register of Historic Places. "Canon Pintado Historic District." Washington, D.C.: Keeper of the Register, 1973. Unpublished Document.

Platt, Kenneth B. "The Taylor Grazing Act in Operation." MS in Western History Collection, University of Colorado, Boulder, Colorado. 17 Articles.

U.S. Forest Service. "History of the Routt Forest." MS at Routt Forest Ranger Station, Steamboat Springs, Colorado, 1972.

Interviews

Interview with Henry Grandt, Craig, Colorado 1978.

Printed Journals

Chavez, Angelico (tr.) and Ted Warner (ed.). *The Dominguez-Escalante Journal.* Provo, Utah: Brigham Young University Press, 1976.

Jackson, Donald and Mary Lee Spence (Eds.). *The Expeditions of John Charles Fremont.* Urbana: University of Illinois Press, 1970.

Nevins, Allan (ed.), *Narratives of Exploration and Adventure by John C. Fremont.* New York: Longmans Green and Co., 1956.

Tice, John H. *Over the Plains, On the Mountains.* London: n.p. 1872.

Townshend, Frederick T. *10,000 Miles of Travel, Sport and Adventure.* London: n.p., 1869.

Wislizenus, F. A. *A Journey to the Rocky Mountains in the Year 1869.* St. Louis: n.p., 1912.

Government Documents

Beekly, A. L. *Geology and Coal Resources of North Park, Colorado.* Washington, D.C.: Government Printing Office, 1915.

Campbell, Marius R. *The Twentymile Park District of the Yampa Coal Field, Routt County, Colorado.* Washington, D.C.: Government Printing Office, 1923.

Colorado Bureau of Mines. "Oil Shales of Colorado." Bulletin. Denver: n.p., 1919.

_____. *The Oil Shales of Northwestern Colorado.* Denver: Eames, 1919.

Fenneman, Nevin M. *The Yampa Coal Fields, Routt County, Colorado.* Washington, D.C.: Government Printing Office, 1906.

Gale, Hoyt S. *Coal Fields of Northwestern Colorado and Northeastern Utah.* Washington, D.C.: Government Printing Office, 1910.

George, R.C. *Coal, Oil Shale and Hydrocarbons on the Denver Northwestern and Pacific Railroad.* Washington, D.C. (Denver): n.p., 1918.

Hancock, E. T. *Geology and Coal Resources of the Axial and Monument Butte Quadrangles of Moffat County, Colorado.* Washington, D.C.: Government Printing Office, 1925.

Hayden, Ferdinand V. *U.S. Geologic Survey of the Territories, Annual Report. 1st-12th. 1867-78.* Washington, D.C.: Government Printing Office, 1968-83.

Lee, Ronald F. *The Antiquities Act of 1906.* Washington, D.C.: National Park Service, 1970.

Meeker, Nathan. *Letter to the Secretary of the Interior, 1879.* Washington, D.C.: Government Printing Office, 1880.

Powell, John W. *Report on the Lands of the Arid Region of the United States.* Washington, D.C.: Government Printing Office, 1879.

Sears, J.D. *Relations of the Wasatch and Green River Formation in Northwestern Colorado and Southern Wyoming,* Washington, D.C.: Government Printing Office, 1924.

State of Colorado. *Publicly Owned Lands in Northwestern Colorado and Northeastern Utah.* Denver: n.p., 1919.

_____. State Board of Immigration. *Colorado: Mineral, Oil and Shale Resources.* Denver: n.p., 1925.

_____. *Colorado's Northwestern Plateau.* Denver: n.p. 1930.

_____. "Cooperative Oil Shale Investigation." Bulletin. Number 1, Boulder, Colo.: State of Colorado, 1921.

_____. *Oil and Gas Statistics, 1974.* Colorado Oil and Gas Conservation Commission, 1975.

U.S. Congress. Committee on Indian Affairs. *Testimony in Relation to the Ute. . . .* Washington, D.C.: Government Printing Office, 1880.

_____. White River Commission, 45th Congress, 2nd

_____. White River Commission, 46th Congress, 2nd Session. Ex. Doc. 83, 1880.

U.S. Department of the Interior, Bureau of Land Management, *Final Environmental Impact Statement, Northwest Colorado Coal.* Denver: Bureau of Land Management, 1975.

_____. *Northwest Supplemental Report.* Denver: Bureau of Land Management, 1978.

_____. *Green River-Hams Fork Regional Coal Environmental Impact Statement.* Denver: Bureau of Land Management, 1980. 2 Vols.

_____. *Draft Environmental Statement, Proposed Superior Oil Company Land Exchange and Oil Shale Resource Development.* Denver: Bureau of Land Management, 1979.

Winchester, Dean E. *Oil Shale in Northwestern Colorado and Adjacent Areas.* Washington, D.C.: Government Printing Office, 1916.

Woodruff, E. G. *Oil Shale of Northwestern Colorado and Northeastern Utah.* Washington, D.C.: Government Printing Office, 1914.

SECONDARY SOURCES

Books

Alter, Cecil James Bridger Trapper. *Columbus, Ohio:* Longs College Book Co., 1951.

Abbott, Carl. *Colorado,* Boulder, Colo.: CAUP. 1976.

Ambos, John. *McCoy Memories.* n. 1., m.p., 1976.

Athearn, Robert G. *Rebel of the Rockies.* New Haven: Yale, 1962.

_____. *The Coloradans.* Albuquerque: University of New Mexico Press, 1976.

Ault, Perry. *From Oxen to Jet Planes.* Steamboat Springs, Colo.: Steamboat Pilot, 1971.

Bailey, Adah. *History of Jackson County, Colorado.* Walden, Colorado: Jackson County *Star.* 1946.

Bartlett, Richard. *Great Surveys of the American West.* Norman: University of Oklahoma Press. 1962.

Berkhofer, Robert. *Salvation and the Savage.* Seattle: University of Washington Press, 1965.

Bender, Henry E. *The Uintah Railway: The Gilsonite Route.* Berkeley, California: Howell-North, 1970.

Black, Robert C. *Island in the Rockies.* Boulder, Colorado: Pruett Press, 1969.

Blackmore, William. *Colorado: Its Resources and Prospects.* London: n.p. 1869.

Billington, Ray A. *Westward Expansion.* New York: MacMillan, 1974.

Bollinger, Edward T. *Rails That Climb: The Story of the Moffat Road.* Santa Fe, New Mexico: Rydal Press, 1950.

Bollinger, Edward T. and Frederick Bauer. *The Moffat Road.* Chicago: Swallow Press, 1962.

122

Bolton, Herbert E. *Pageant in the Wilderness, The Story of the Escalante Expedition to the Interior Basin, 1776.* Salt Lake City: Utah State Historical Society, 1950.

Boner, Harold. *The Giant's Ladder: David H. Moffat and His Railroad.* Milwaukee: Kalmbach Publishing Co., 1962.

Boyd, J. P. *Recent Indian Wars.* n.1., n.p., 1891.

Bowen, A. W. *Progessive Men of Western Colorado.* Chicago: A. W. Bowen and Co., 1905.

Bowles, Samuel. *The Switzerland of America, A Summer Vacation in the Parks and Mountains of Colorado.* New York: n.p., 1869.

_____. *Our New West.* New York: n.p., 1869.

Brown, Margaret. *Shepherdess of the Elk River Valley.* Denver: Golden Bell Press, 1967.

Burroughs, John Rolfe. *Where the Old West Stayed Young.* New York: Morrow, 1962.

_____. *Guardian of the Grasslands: The First 100 Years of the Wyoming Stockgrowers Association.* Cheyenne: Pioneer Printing and Stationery Co., 1971.

_____. *Steamboat in the Rockies.* Fort Collins, Colorado: Old Army Press, 1974.

Bury, Susan and John. *This is What I Remember.* Meeker, Colorado: Rio Blanco Historical Society, 1972.

Cairns, Mary L. *Grand Lake: The Pioneers.* Denver: World Press, 1946.

_____. *The Olden Days, A Companion Book to Grand Lake: The Pioneers.* Denver: World Press, 1952.

Campbell, John A. *Indian Echoes. . . .* Denver: n.p., 1970. Reprint of 1905 edition.

Canfield, John G. *Mines and Mining Men of Colorado.* n.1., n.p., 1893.

Carson, Christopher "Kit." *Autobiography.* Chicago: Lakeside Press, 135.

Corregan, Robert A. and David F. Livgane. *Colorado Mining Directory.* Denver: Colorado Mining Directory Co., 1883.

Crofutt, George A. *A Grip-Sack Guide to Colorado.* Omaha: Overland Publishing Co., 1881.

d'Azevedo, Warren L., et al. *The Current Status of Anthropological Research in the Great Basin, 1964.* Reno: Desert Research Institute, 1966.

Dawson, Thomas F. *The Ute War.* Boulder, Colorado: Johnson Publishing Co., 1964. Reprint of 1879 version.

Donelson, Alice R. *The North Park Stockgrowers, 1899-1970.* Steamboat Springs, Colorado: Steamboat *Pilot,* 1973.

Dorsett, Lyle. *The Queen City - A History of Denver.* Boulder, Colo.: Pruett, 1977.

Drago, Harry S. *The Great Range Wars: Violence on the Grasslands.* New York: Dodds, Mead and Co., 1970.

Ellison, W. H. (Ed.). *Life and Adventures of George Nidever.* Berkeley, California: University of California Press, 1937.

Emmitt, Robert. *The Last War Trail, The Utes and the Settlement of Colorado.* Norman: University of Oklahoma Press, 1954.

Ewing, Clark C. and Pamela Berude and Margaret C. Ewing. *Early McCoy, A Hundred Years Perspective.* Glenwood Springs, Colo.: Raymond's Printers, 1976.

Fiester, Mark. *Blasted, Beloved Breckenridge.* Boulder, Colorado: Pruett Press, 1973.

Fisher, Frank. *Our Future Oil Resources.* n.1., n.p., 1925.

Fossett, Frank. *History of Colorado.* Denver: *Daily Tribune,* 1876.

_____. *Colorado: Its Gold and Silver Mines, Farms and Stock Ranges, Health and Pleasure Resorts.* New York: Crawford, 1879.

Frink, Maurice. *When Grass Was King.* Boulder, Colorado: University of Colorado Press, 1956.

Frost, David M. *Notes on General Ashley.* Barre, Mass.: Barre *Gazette,* 1960.

Grady, James. *Environmental Factors in Archaeological Site Location, Piceance Basin, Colorado.* Denver: Bureau of Land Management, 1980.

Goetzmann, William H. *Army Exploration in the American West.* New Haven: Yale University Press, 1951.

_____. *Exploration and Empire.* New York: Knopf, 1964.

Hafen, LeRoy. *Colorado and Its People.* New York: Lewis Historical Publishing Co., 1948.

_____. (ed.). *The Mountain Men and the Fur Trade of the Far West.* Glendale, California.

Hall, Frank. *History of the State of Colorado.* Chicago: Blakely Printing, 1895. 4 Volumes.

Harrison, Louise C. *Empire and the Berthoud Pass.* Denver: Bit Mountain Press, 1964.

Hayden, Ferdinand V. *The Great West.*, Bloomington, Illinois: C. R. Brodix, 1880.

Henderson, C. W. *Mining in Colorado.* Boulder, Colorado: University of Colorado Press, 1926.

Hughel, Avvon Chew. *The Chew Bunch in Brown's Park.* San Francisco: Scrimshaw Press. 1970.

Incoporation of the Natural and Industrial Exposition Association. Colorado Condensed. n.l., n.p. 1881.

Ingersoll, Ernest. *Knocking Around the Rockies.* London: n.p., 1883.

Jocknick, Sidney. *Early Days on the Western Slope.* Denver: Carson-Harper, 1913.

Kimball, Maria B. *A Soldier-Doctor of Our Army.* N. 1., n.p., 1917.

La Baw, Wallace. *Noh-oon-Kara: The Gold of Breckenridge.* Denver: Big Mountain Press, 1965.

La Messena, Robert A. *Rio Grande...To The Pacific.* Denver: Sundance Limited, 1975. 2nd Edition.

Leckenby, Charles H. *The Tread of Pioneers.* Steamboat Springs, Colorado: Steamboat *Pilot,* 1944.

Look, Al. *The Utes Last Stand at White River and Milk Creek, Western Colorado in 1879.* Denver: Golden Bell Press, 1972.

Mc Intoch, James. *Compendium of Oil Shale Literature from 1863 to Present.* n.l., n.p., 1967.

Mc Mechen, Edgar C. *The Moffat Tunnel of Colorado.* Denver: Wahlgren Publishing Co., 1927. 2 Volumes.

McQueary, Lela. *Widening Trails: Narrative of Pioneer Days in Middle Park.* Denver: World Press, 1962.

Mallory, William W. *Geologic Atlas of the Rocky Mountain Region.* Denver: Rocky Mountain Association of Petroleum Geologists, 1972.

Meeker, Josephine. *The Ute Massacre.* Philadelphia: Old Franklin Publishing Co., 1879.

Merritt, Wesley. *Merritt and the Indian Wars.* London: Johnson-Trauton Military Press, 1972.

Mills, Enos A. *The Rocky Mountain National Park. Estes Park, Colorado.*, n.p., 1932.

Miner, Agnes F. *Founding and Early History of Breckenridge, Colorado.* Denver: n.p., n.d.

Morgan, Dale L. *Jedediah Smith and the Opening of the West.* Lincoln: University of Nebraska Press, 1955.

_____. (ed.). *The West of William H. Ashley.* Denver: Old West Publishing Co., 1965.

Osgood, Ernest S. *The Day of the Cattlemen.* Chicago: University of Chicago Press, 1929.

Parkhill, Forbes. *The Wildest of the West.* Denver: Sage, 1957.

Pauly, Nell. *Grand Lake, Ghosts of the Shootin'.* Grand Lake, Colorado: n.p., 1961.

Payne, Steven. *Where the Rockies Ride Herd.* Denver: Sage, 1965.

Peake, Ora B. *The Colorado Range Cattle Industry.* Glendale, California: A. H. Clark, 1937.

Poor, M. Clarence. *Denver, South Park and Pacific.* Denver: Rocky Mountain Railroad Club, 1949.

Prucha, Francis Paul. *Guide to Military Posts.* Madison: Wisconsin State Historical Society, 1964.

Quaife, Milson M. (ed.). *Kit Carson's Autobiography.* Lincoln: University of Nebraska Press, 1936 (Lakeside Press Edition).

Rankin, M. Wilson. *Reminiscences of Frontier Days...*n.1., n.p., 1935.

Sage, Rufus B. *His Letters and Papers.* Glendale, California: A. H. Clark, 1956.

_____. *Rocky Mountain Life.* Glendale, California: A. H. Clark, 1956.

Sprague, Marshall. *Massacre: Tragedy at White River.* Boston: Little, Brown, 1957.

Stevenson, Thelma. V. *Historic Hahn's Peak.* Ft. Collins, Colo.: n.p., 1976.

Stegner, Wallace. *This is Dinosaur.* New York: Knopf, 1955.

_____. (ed.). *U.S. Geographical and Geological Survey of the Rocky Mountain Region.* Cambridge, Mass.: Harvard University Press, 1962. (The Powell survey report).

Steinel, Alvin T. *History of Agriculture in Colorado.* Fort Collins, Colorado: Colorado A and M University, 1926.

Stone, Wilbur F. *History of Colorado.* Denver: S. J. Clarke and Co., 1918. 4 Volumes.

Tonge, Thomas. *The "Moffat Road."* Denver: n.p., 1906.

_____. *Handbook of Colorado Resources.* Denver: Smith Brooks, 1907.

Thayer, William. *Marvels of the New West.* New York: n.p., 1887.

Thwaites, Reuben G. (ed.). *Travels in the Far Northwest.* Cleveland: A. H. Clark, 1906.

Ubbelohde, Carl, Maxine Benson, and Duane Smith. *A History of Colorado:* Pruett Press, 1976.

Verplanck, J. D. *A Glimpse of Arcadia and Beyond.* n.1., n.p., 1938.

Vestal, Stanley. *Jim Bridger, Mountain Man.* Lincoln: University of Nebraska Press, 1946.

_____. *Joe Meek, The Merry Mountain Man.* Lincoln: University of Nebraska Press, 1952.

_____. *The Mountain Men.* Boston: Houghton, Mifflin, 1937.

Weston, William. *The Yampa Coal Field of Routt County, Colorado.* Denver: n.p., 1907.

Worster, Donald. *The Dust Bowl.* New York: Oxford University Press, 1979.

_____ "Egeria Park As I Remember It." *Colorado Magazine.* XL, No. 4, 1963. pp. 300-309.

Pamphlets

Author Unknown. *Colorado's Western Mountain Region.* Denver: Colorado. Colorado Interstate Gas Co., 1965.

Colorado State Commercial Association. *The White-Bear River Country, An Undeveloped Empire.* Denver: Smith-Brooks, 1907.

Federated Commercial Clubs of Northwest Colorado. *An Imperial Empire: Northwestern Colorado.* Steamboat Springs, Colorado: Steamboat *Pilot,* 1924.

Hayden Townsite Company. *A Message From Hayden.* Denver: Smith-Brooks, 1912.

Laramie, Hahn's Peak and Pacific Railroad. *The Wonderful North Park Coal Field: The Yampa Coal Field.* Laramie: n.p., 1911.

Oak Creek *Times.* Centennial Edition. *Oak Creek, Colorado:* Steamboat *Pilot,* 1926.

Moffat Tunnel District Development Association. *Resource Edition, Steamboat Springs, Colorado:* Steamboat *Pilot,* 1926.

Moffat Tunnel League. *Northwestern Colorado Prosperity and Resource Edition.* Steamboat Springs, Colorado: Steamboat *Pilot,* 1927.

Rio Grande Industries. *Annual Report.* Denver: RGI, 1979.

Newspapers

Denver *Daily News.* October 13, 1879.

Denver *Post.* September 4, 1930. Great Divide Barbecue.

_____ Olga Curtis. "Farrington Carpenter, The Success Story of a 'Failure'." April 11, 1965 and April 18, 1965.

_____ November 9, 1969. Coalmont, Colorado, in North Park.

_____ September 17, 1972. "Butch Cassidy's Early Exploits Recalled."

Georgetown *Courier*. 1886, "Among the Silver Seams."

Meeker *Herald*. January 14, 1888.

Steamboat *Pilot*. August 19, 1976. "Hayden Celebrates a Birthday."

Theses and Dissertations

Athearn, Frederic J. "Life and Society in Eighteenth Century New Mexico, 1695-1776." Austin: University of Texas, 1974. Ph.D Dissertation.

Crowley, John M. "Ranches in the Sky." Minneapolis: University of Minnesota, 1964. Ph.D Dissertation.

Hamann, R. E. "A Bibliography of the Cultural Development in Northwestern Colorado." Boulder: University of Colorado, n. d., M.A. Thesis.

Iden, T. L. "History of the Ute Indian Cessions of Colorado." Gunnison, Colorado: Western State College, 1928. M.A. Thesis.

Nixon, Elizabeth. "The Meeker Massacres." Greeley, Colorado: Colorado State Teachers College, 1935. M.A. Thesis.

Ottens, Emily Marie. "An Economic Analysis of the Resources and Development Potential for Mottat, Rio Blanco and Routt Counties in Northwestern Colorado." Boulder: University of Colorado, 1957. M.A. Thesis.

Oberholtzer, Cora Belle. "The Grazing Industry of Middle Park, Colorado." Boulder: University of Colorado, 1942. M.A. Thesis.

Perini, V. C. "Oil Reconnaissance in Northwestern Colorado." Boulder: University of Colorado, n.d. M.A. Thesis.

Spiva, Agnes E. "The Utes in Colorado." Boulder: University of Colorado, 1929. M.A. Thesis.

Tyler, Daniel. "F. R. Carpenter, Routt County, 1900-20" Fort Collins: Colorado State University, 1967. M.A. Thesis.

Articles

R. E. Arnett. "Ranching in Northwest Colorado in the Early Eighties." *Colorado Magazine.* XX, No. 6, 1943, pp. 202-224.

Author, unknown. "The Middle Park Claim Club." *Colorado Magazine.* X, 5, 1933, pp. 189-194.

Bailey, Adah. "Montie Blevins, North Park Cattleman". *Colorado Magazine.* VXIII, No. 1, 1941, pp. 13-18.

Carr, L. H. "Early Mining in Colorado." *Outwest Magazine.* June, 1922.

Collum, Joseph S. "Experiences in the Bear River Country in the 1870s." *Colorado Magazine.* XI, No. 4, 1934, pp. 153-159.

Easton, Frank A. "Enterprise at Fraser." *Denver Westerners Brand Book.* Denver, 1954. pp. 120-138.

Flynn, A. J. "Fur and Forts of the Rocky Mountain West." *Colorado Magazine.* IX, No. 2, 1932, pp. 45-47.

_____. "Furs and Forts of the Rocky Mountain West." *Colorado Magazine.* X, No. 6, 1932, pp. 45-57.

Fradkin, Philip L. "Craig, Colorado: Population Unknown, Elevation 6,185 Feet," *Audubon.* July, 1977, Vol. 79, No. 4.

Hafen, Leroy R. "Fraeb's Last Fight and How Battle Creek Got Its Name," *Colorado Magazine.* VII, No. 3, 1930, pp. 97-102.

_____. "The Counties of Colorado: A History of Their Creation and the Origin of Their Names." *Colorado Magazine.* VXV, No. 2, 1932, pp. 27-60.

_____. "The Coming of the Automobile and Improved Roads to Colorado." *Colorado Magazine.* VIII, No. 1, 1931, pp. 1-17.

_____. "With Fur Traders in Colorado, 1839-40: The Journal of E. Willard Smith:." *Colorado Magazine.* XXVII, No. 3, 1950, pp. 161-188.

_____. "Fort Davy Crockett." *Colorado Magazine.* XXIX, No. 10, 1952, pp. 17-33.

_____. "The Sinclair-Bean Party of Trappers." 1830-32. *Colorado Magazine.* XXXI, No. 3, 1954, pp. 161-172.

Hampton, H. D. "Four with Grinell in North Park." *Colorado Magazine.* XLVIII, No. 4, 1971, pp. 273-299.

Harmon, E. M. "The Story of the Indian Fort Near Granby, Colorado." *Colorado Magazine.* XXII, No. 4, 1945, pp. 167-171.

_____. "The Mail Carriers Substitute." *The Trail.* II, No. 3, 1909. p. 13. (Regarding the Killing of Tabernash).

_____. "Early Days in Middle Park." *Colorado Magazine.* XV, No. 5, 1938, pp. 54-63.

Hayden, Ferdinand V. "Explorations Made in Colorado Under the Direction of Professor Ferdinand V. Hayden in 1876." *American Naturalist.* XI, No. 2, 1877. pp. 73-86.

Harvey, Mr. and Mrs. James R. "'Squeaky' Bob Wheeler's Hunting and Ranch Life." *Colorado Magazine.* XXIV, No. 4, 1947, pp. 145-158.

Hill, Mrs. C. P. "The Beginnings of Rangely and How the First School Teacher Came to Town." *Colorado Magazine.* XI, No. 3, 1934. pp. 112-116.

Jerome, John L. "A Camping Trip to Northwestern Colorado in 1875." *Colorado Magazine* XIX, No. 5, 1942, pp. 167-175.

Leach, Richard E. "Colorow." *The Trail.* V, No. 4, 1912. p. 22.

Leckenby, Charles H. "The Founding of Steamboat Springs and of Hahn's Peak." *Colorado Magazine.* VI, No. 3, 1929, pp. 92-98.

_____. "The Discovery of Gold at Hahn's Peak and the Tragic Death of Joseph Hahn." *Tread of Pioneers.* 1944.

_____. "Unrest of the Utes: Why the Ute Indians Lost Their Heritage." *Tread of Pioneers.* 1944.

Londoner, Wolfe. "Colorow: Renegade Chief Dines Out." *Colorado Magazine.* IX, No. 3, 1932, pp. 93-95.

Merritt, Wesley. "Three Indian Campaigns." *Harpers Weekly.* April, 1890. pp. 720-737.

Mitchell, Guy E. "Billions of Barrels of Oil Locked Up in the Rockies." *National Geographic.* February, 1918.

Morris, Ernest. "A Glimpse of Moffat Tunnel History." *Colorado Magazine.* IV, No. 2, 1927, pp. 63-66.

Mory, Guy E. "The Pueblo Flood of 1921." *Colorado Magazine.* XVII, No. 6, 1940, pp. 274-286.

Nankivell, John. "Colorado's Last Indian War." *Colorado Magazine.* XI, No. 3, 1934, pp. 222-234.

Neiman, Charles W. "The Lu Baggs Ranch." *Colorado Magazine.* XXIII, 1946, pp. 105-114.

Oldham, Mary D. "Sixty Seven Years in the White River Valley." *Colorado Magazine.* XXIX, No. 3, 1952, pp. 195-201.

Parsons, Eugene. "Farnham's Western Travels." *The Trail.* VII, No. 3, 1914, p. 10.

Payne, John T. "Early Days in North Park, Colorado." *Colorado Magazine.* XIV, No. 6, 1937, pp. 230-232.

Payne, Steven. "Recollections of North Park." *Westerners Brandbook.* Denver 1946.

Pearl, Richard M. "Gem Mining in Colorado." *Colorado Magazine.* XVI, No. 6, 1939, pp. 218-221.

Pierce, Elladean. "Early Days of Craig, Colorado." *Colorado Magazine.* V, No. 4, 1928, pp. 152-159.

Potts, Merlin K. "Rocky Mountain National Park." *Colorado Magazine.* XLII, No. 3, 1965, pp. 216-224.

Quinn, Elizabeth. "Perilous Adventure of a North Park Pioneer Woman, Mrs. L. A. Gresham." *Colorado Magazine.* XVI, No. 4, 2939, pp. 143-146.

Ronzio, Richard A. "The Uintah Railroad: The Gilsonite Road." *Westerners Brandbook.* Denver, 1959.

Robinson, A. A. "Recollections of Craig." *Colorado Magazine* XIX, No. 2, 1942, pp. 62-73.

Rollins, John Q. A., Jr. "John Q. A. Rollins, Colorado Builder." *Colorado Magazine.* XVI, No. 3, 1939, pp. 110-119.

Shoemaker, Len. "National Forests." *Colorado Magazine*. XX, No. 5, 1944, pp. 182-184.

Shelton, William. "The Threshing Machine for the Meeker Indian Agency." *Colorado Magazine*. IX, No. 5, 1932, pp. 217-218.

Sims, W. D. "The Founding and Founders of Meeker." *Colorado Magazine*. XXVI, No. 4, 1949, pp. 271-277.

Sons of Colorado. *Sons of Colorado*. II, No. 8, 1908. p. 13. (Note on Moffat Road).

Stegner, Wallace. "Jack Sumner and J.W. Powell." *Colorado Magazine*. XXVI, No. 2, 1949, pp. 61-69.

Taylor, David. "To the Bear River Country in 1883." *Colorado Magazine*. XXXI, No. 2, 1954, pp. 119-128.

Thomas, Chauncy. "Some Characteristics of Jim Baker." *Colorado Magazine*. IV, No. 4, 1929, pp. 146-157.

Toll, Roger W. "The Hayden Survey in Colorado in 1873-1874." *Colorado Magazine*. VI, No. 4, 1929, pp. 146-157.

Trail, The. "The Pioneers of Routt County." *The Trail*. I, No. 2, 1908, pp. 16-17.

_____. "Irving Hale's Trip Through Middle Park." *The Trail*. I, No. 2, 1908, pp. 30-35 and No. 4, pp. 3-10.

_____. *The Trail*. XIV, No. 20, 1922. p. 24, (Oil Creek Mentioned).

Watson, Elmo S. "John W. Powell's Colorado Expedition of 1867." *Colorado Magazine*. XXVII, No. 4, 1950. pp. 303-312.

Wentworth, Edward N. "Sheep Wars of the '90s in Northwest Colorado." *Westerners Brandbook*. Denver, 1946.

Wolcott, Frank H. "Monarch of Grand County." *Westerners Brandbook*. Denver, 1954.

Willis, Ann Bassett. "Queen Ann of Brown's Park." *Colorado Magazine*. XXIX, No. 2, 1952, pp. 81-88. XXIC, No. 3, 1952, pp. 218-235, and XXX, No. 1, 1953, pp. 58-77.

Wilson, Mary Adella King. "We Move to Egeria Park." *Colorado Magazine*. XL, No. 2, 1963, pp. 121-128.

ABOUT THE AUTHOR

Frederic J. Athearn was born in Minnesota, but has lived in Colorado since 1946 where he attended the University of Colorado receiving a B.A. in History. He pursued graduate work at St. Louis University and was awarded a M.A. in History and Spanish. He earned a Ph.D at the University of Texas at Austin specializing in New Mexican and Western American History. He lectured at the University of Texas and the University of Colorado where he taught U.S. History, Western American History, and Colorado History.

The author is presently the Bureau of Land Management's Colorado State Office Historian, a position he has occupied since 1975. The author has published in numerous professional journals and is a member of various professional history societies.